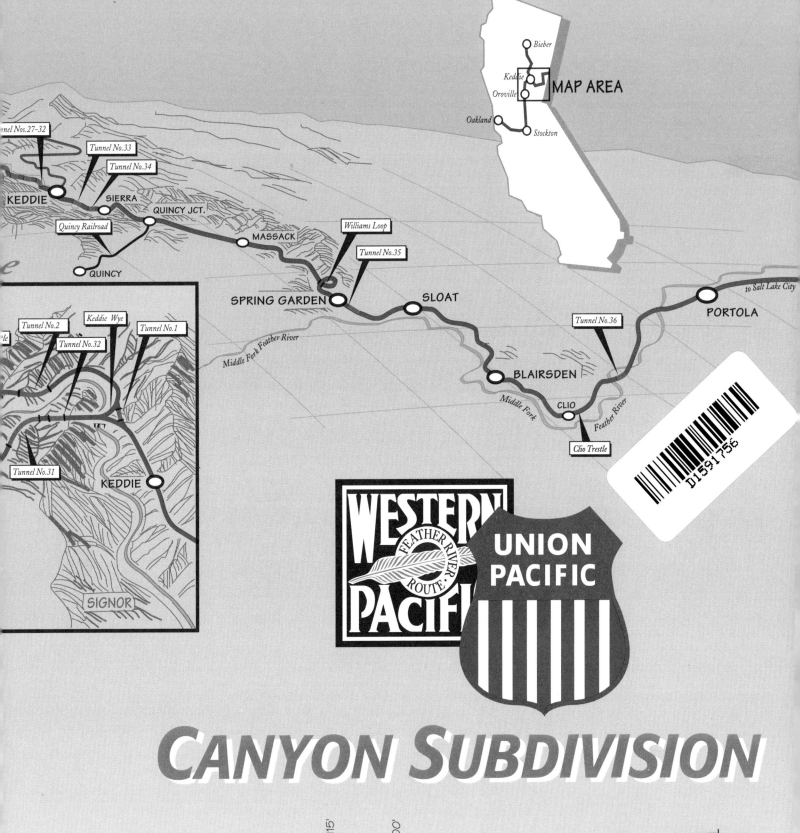

MAP AREA

Bieber
Keddie
Oroville
Oakland
Stockton

Tunnel Nos.27-32
Tunnel No.33
Tunnel No.34
KEDDIE
SIERRA
Quincy Railroad
QUINCY JCT.
QUINCY
MASSACK
Williams Loop
Tunnel No.35
SPRING GARDEN
SLOAT
Tunnel No.36
PORTOLA
to Salt Lake City
Middle Fork Feather River
BLAIRSDEN
Middle Fork
CLIO
Feather River
Clio Trestle

Tunnel No.2
Keddie Wye
Tunnel No.1
Tunnel No.32
Tunnel No.31
KEDDIE
SIGNOR

WESTERN PACIFIC — FEATHER RIVER ROUTE

UNION PACIFIC

CANYON SUBDIVISION

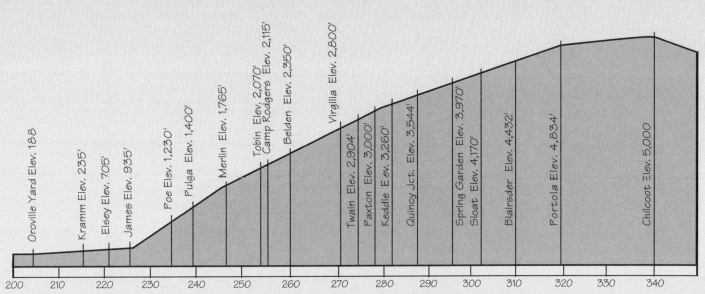

Oroville Yard Elev. 188
Kramm Elev. 235'
Elsey Elev. 705'
James Elev. 935'
Poe Elev. 1,230'
Pulga Elev. 1,400'
Merlin Elev. 1,765'
Tobin Elev. 2,070'
Camp Rodgers Elev. 2,115'
Belden Elev. 2,350'
Virgilia Elev. 2,800'
Twain Elev. 2,904'
Paxton Elev. 3,000'
Keddie Elev. 3,260'
Quincy Jct. Elev. 3,544'
Spring Garden Elev. 3,970'
Sloat Elev. 4,170'
Blairsden Elev. 4,432'
Portola Elev. 4,834'
Chilcoot Elev. 5,000'

200   210   220   230   240   250   260   270   280   290   300   310   320   330   340

D159 1756

THE
FEATHER RIVER CANYON

Union Pacific's Heart of Stone

Steve Schmollinger

Pentrex • Pasadena, California

Front cover:
An MINPV (Milpitas - North Platte vehicles) approaches tunnel 9 on March 1, 1996, just as late-afternoon shadows engulf the right-of-way. The eastbound has just passed Maintenance of Way (M of W) crews and equipment working the siding at Poe. Below and out of sight is the Feather River, which makes a large bend to get around the base of Hungry Hunt Peak through which the tunnel passes. The 70 F weather in the lower part of the canyon signals the coming of spring. However, by the time the MINPV's T-shirted crew detrains at Portola, 80 miles up the line, the moon will be up and the temperature 40 degrees lower.

Rear cover:
A westbound Union Pacific unit grain train has a clear block below Pulga as it illuminates the slide fence above the river. Were a significant part of the mountain lurking above the train to give way, the slide fence would do little but add to the debris pushing hoppers into the water a hundred feet below.

False title page:
The canyon is full of waterfalls and cataracts as an OAAP6 pierces the Honeymoon Tunnels. At times, the heavy rains of winter and spring 1995 turned the canyon into a "Waterworld" nightmare for both UP and Caltrans. Shortly after this scene of snow-melt wending its way down the steep precipice next to the tracks was captured on film, the cataracts and high water vanished.

Title page:
In June 1974, Western Pacific 728 is switching the yard at Portola as five Union Pacific U30Cs pull in after an early-morning run up the Feather River Canyon. The U-boats went down the canyon the night before and were quickly turned at Stockton for the return trip east. In eight and one-half years, Western Pacific will be merged into the UP.

Frontispiece (opposite title page):
On March 2, 1996, at 3:47 p.m., 9562 West, an APOA (American President Lines Chicago - Oakland) double-stack container train, rounds the bare granite slopes at tunnel 9 near Jarbo (between Poe and Pulga). The portal of tunnel 10 is visible up the line about one and one-half miles. The train passed Keddie around noon, and it's been slow-going ever since because of M of W and a meet with an OAAP6 led by a Chicago & North Western C44-9W at Belden. An STMET (Stockton - Memphis trailers), with another "lightning-stripe" C44 leading, was the first train through here this afternoon and headed for Merlin for a meet with two westbounds, an NPOAV (North Platte - Oakland vehicles) and the close-running APOA. Train 3800 East, an STNP (Stockton - North Platte manifest), passed next and headed in at Pulga for both westbounds; it'd meet two more at Camp Rodgers. The weather is gorgeous—near 70 F. There's lots of water in the river; a couple are fishing about 300 feet below in a large pool that helps form a large bend in the river. Near the west end of the tunnel, water coming off the mountainside percolates under the coal-black ballast and trickles over the edge toward the river—there's no culvert. On the east, a huge, bare, multi-colored granite rock face stares down on trains that are protected only by a slide fence. Water is coming down both sides of the canyon in countless thousand-foot cascades. Foreman Audy Van Zant and his M of W crew and their high-tech machinery, including a huge "Super CAT" tamper, are continuing the track maintenance they were doing yesterday at Poe and up the line toward Pulga. Calvin, the Canyon Sub dispatcher on duty in Omaha this afternoon, is having to juggle track-and-time permits with M of W forces and signal maintainers all along the canyon line. There are so many crews working that they often "walk" on each other trying to contact Calvin at the same time. Near Camp Rodgers, a slide fence has malfunctioned, requiring train crews to flag red signals and slowing movements to a crawl. The signal crew that's just reached the fence can't get enough time between trains to connect the 15 strands of wire required to complete the repairs; they'll have to wait another day. Calvin tells them, "Better luck tomorrow."

Library of Congress Cataloging-in-Publication Data

Schmollinger, Steve.
    The Feather River Canyon : Union Pacific's heart
of stone / Steve Schmollinger.
       p. cm.
    ISBN 1-56342-005-8 (alk. paper)
    1. Union Pacific Railroad Company. 2. Railroads-
-California--Feather River Valley. I. Title.
TF25.U5S36 1996   96-42300
385'.09794--dc20   CIP

Two UP "comfort-cab" diesels, one built by General Electric and the other by General Motors, lead a westbound double-stack train out of Portola. The train's destination is the Port of Oakland, 312 miles and another crew change away.

As the sun climbs and moves west, one can see shadows move in tandem on the rock face beyond the sweeping curve below Virgilia. Standing at the same location for nearly an hour reveals just how rapidly the shadows move across the granite, which turns from an amorphous black mass to a well-defined, detailed surface as light hits it. Into the curve comes UP 6073 East, ducking in and out of shadows all the way from Intake to Portola. The crew seems spellbound when they spot the photographer's 500mm optic across the river reflecting the colors of their SD60.

Notes and Acknowledgments

First of all, I'd like to thank my Heavenly Father for His unseen but ever-present support in preparing this book. It's only through His power that I've learned to operate a camera and put it to some use. We're only here for a short time, and I thank Him that I had the opportunity to regularly photograph one of the most beautiful and serene places within striking distance of my home.

Next, I'd like to express my appreciation to my wife, Lynn, and my five energetic young children, Alex, Burke, Carlyle, Wyatte, and Mia. I'm one of those lucky men who's married to a lady who supports me in many ways while I attempt to create with the camera. Only those who are married can understand how key a supportive and talented spouse is to such a project as this. Most of the fun putting this volume together came as my family enjoyed the sights and sounds of the canyon and railroad with me. Although keeping one eye on our children to make sure they didn't fall over a cliff or into the river while attempting to concentrate on the photograph at hand was often nerve-racking, I treasure the fact that we witnessed those scenes together.

I'm grateful to all the photographers who submitted photographs for possible use in this book. Each one of those photos, whether or not they were ultimately used, represents considerable effort and creativity on the part of the photographer. I appreciate the time each of those individuals took from his hectic schedule to gather photos together, carefully package them, and send them to me at his own expense. The photographers whose work does appear in the book are Eric Blasko, Mark Bordine, Dave Burton, Tom Danneman, Brian Jennison, Fred Matthews, Wayne Monger, Tom Mongouvan, Dave Stanley, Brian Solomon, James Speaker, Randy Woods, and Sean Zwagerman.

If one thing came ringing through after rigorously observing operations on the Feather River line, it's that Union Pacific is a class act. John Bromley, the railroad's PR man, gave tireless help in obtaining permission for me to photograph on the property, obtaining train line-ups, and information on the legendary 6900s. I hope I have the chance to work with John again in the future.

Ted Benson's black-and-white masterpiece, *Echoes Down the Canyon*, served as partial inspiration for this all-color volume. Although he probably doesn't recall, I was standing next to him when he made the exposure

of UP 6908 West that graces the cover of his book. We'd happened upon Ted and Dave Styffe as we chased the D-D off the desert. After pacing the 6908 down the canyon, I, along with Ted, Dave, Lynn Powell, and Gary Holmes, witnessed the big Centennial change crews at Oroville in twilight and then rocket out of town with its *Overland Mail West* in an impressive show of diesel smoke and instant acceleration. I'd also like to thank two other authors, Dave Stanley and John Walker, for their text which appears as part of this work. Hal Carstens graciously allowed me to reprint Dave's article, "At the Throttle of Elegance," from the December 1994 issue of *Railfan and Railroad*, and Vic Neves did the same for John's article, "Highrailing the Feather River Canyon," which appeared in the August 31, 1990, issue of the *Lark*. John also helped indirectly through his well-researched article, "The Shield and the Feather," published in *Trains*. Dave Stanley proved an indispensable source of information and perspective. His views from the cab give us a feel for the ruggedness, danger, and beauty of the canyon that we would not have had without his camera work. As you look through these pages, you'll undoubtedly notice that he's also expert with the camera when he's not in the cab.

I doubt the "Wisconsin Boys," Don Gulbrandsen and Tom Danneman, knew what they were getting into when they took a trip into the canyon as part of their Winterail 1995 adventure. What an adventure it turned into! Had they been locals, I doubt they would've deliberately entered it, for they would've been aware that, under such stormy conditions, the canyon quickly becomes a tempestuous milieu seemingly deaf to the anxieties of anyone or anything caught in it. I want to thank Don for penning his recollections of their memorable experience.

One of the most interesting parts of photographing railroad operations along the Feather River was observing how locomotive headlights illuminated the details of rock faces in the rugged lower stretch of the canyon between Keddie and Poe. Instead of the huge banks of flashbulbs Dale Sanders and a score of assistants used in 1985 to paint with light the details on and around the North Fork bridge, I was left with only the headlights and ditchlights of locomotives to paint the boulders, fissures, and slide fences in their path. Although my approach was certainly less precise and time-consuming, it nevertheless provided a demonstration of how bright headlights bring the canyon's rocks and trees to life for crews watching vigilantly for obstacles. Another light source I tried to use was the moon, which I and my children witnessed rise in full glory over the tall ridge southeast of Pulga as we awaited and recorded the passing of Union Pacific 683 East.

Left: As light begins to fail, a grain train rolls its heavy tonnage through the west end of Pulga, hundreds of feet below Highway 70. From here to the North Fork bridge, slides are commonplace.

1.
Introduction

The air is moist, the foliage an intense green. As it has for centuries, water flows by your feet in a sylvan setting. The land is rugged and rustic, as though far removed from civilization. All you can clearly hear is a slight breeze passing through the live oak leaves and pine needles and the trickling of water over orange and silver rock. From a distance somewhere beyond the imposing ridge to your right comes a powerful rhythm not native to these environs. As each second passes, anticipation grows, and your attention focuses more keenly on the huge concrete structure in front of you. Finally, with towering columns of steam rising into the clouds, Union Pacific locomotives 844 and 3985 burst out of tunnel 8 onto the North Fork bridge. Their journey through the Feather River Canyon has now begun in earnest!

Higher up in the Sierra, melting snow still clings to the branches of conifers. The "bite" from last night's sub-freezing temperatures is nearly gone, and tiny droplets of water fall steadily to the ground at a frequency directly proportional to the rising air temperature. Eventually the droplets form puddles, which grow larger and larger as more and more moisture falls from the trees and patches of snow, until they combine in an ocean-bound cascade through rivulets and gullies. Rocky soil keeps the moisture from seeping into the ground as it wends its way downhill, allowing ever greater volumes of frigid water to join together. Several miles below, the waters have become a force to be reckoned with, filling the bottom of a canyon they occupy year-round. This is the Feather River and its playground, the Sierra Nevada Mountains. Following the contours of the western slope of the Sierra, the Feather wends its way in several forks to the Sacramento Valley.

For the latter half of the nineteenth century, the only rail line linking northern California and the rest of the country lay through Donner Pass, 45 miles south of the canyon. The Central Pacific had built its legendary line over the mountains in 1867-68 as it struggled eastward to meet the Union Pacific coming across the Plains. But UP wasn't much thrilled with handing traffic off at Ogden, Utah, to the CP (later part of the Southern Pacific), and then watching its freight stall in Donner's heavy snows. It wanted its own, lower route over the spine of the Golden State—assuming one could be found. Thus, in the 1880s, Omaha dispatched surveyor Virgil Bogue to the area to scout the Feather as a possible route to San Francisco. Despite Bogue's successful trip, UP's interest waned.

The way Arthur Keddie saw it, the course that the river followed along the lower contours of the mountains was a prime candidate to host a railroad.

Rather than going over the top of the Sierra, at an elevation above 7,000 feet, why not hug the banks of the river whose elevation, for the most part, stayed well below 4,000? Keddie believed so fervently in his dream of a railroad through the Feather River Canyon that he made his own survey. Before work started on the Central Pacific, Keddie presented his plan for a relatively low crossing of the Sierra Nevada to Southern Pacific's C.P. Huntington, whose disdain was captured in his response that "no one will ever build a railroad through the Feather River Canyon." Huntington was dead wrong. When E.H. Harriman gained control of both UP and SP at the turn of the century, the reality of a Feather River route took one giant step toward reality. George Gould, who controlled the Denver & Rio Grande, saw a railroad through the canyon as his way to break the UP-SP chokehold Harriman had on him at the Ogden Gateway. With the completion of Gould's Western Pacific in 1909, Keddie's dream became a reality. Gould's engineers used much of Keddie's survey, a fact that must have warmed the old man's heart. His dreaming, searching, and surveying had turned into a living, breathing railroad!

When WP merged with Union Pacific in 1982, the Feather River route gained importance not only from the perspective of UP's stockholders, but also from the point of view of customers and other players in the market. Take the Port of Oakland and American President Lines, headquartered in the same city, for example. Oakland is a gateway for international and domestic traffic, and the Port wanted to take full advantage of its location as an easily accessible terminal at the western end of the Central Corridor. To reach this goal, the Port helped fund a project in the mid-1980s to increase clearances in tunnels in the canyon to accommodate two 9' 6" containers stacked on well cars. The project paid off. Over the course of the decade that followed, APL increased the number of its "Liner" trains traversing UP's central corridor from a handful per week to several each day.

Right: UP 844 and 3985 on the North Fork bridge with columns of steam rising skyward. **Dave Stanley**

Above: The squeal of flanges echoes between tall, sheer granite cliffs below Pulga as new Chevy trucks make their way toward the Bay Area. This NPOAV train from North Platte, Neb., has already passed through two dozen tunnels since leaving Portola, and will thread eight more before reaching Oroville.

Opposite page: On August 25, 1982, BN 137 descends the canyon through the Honeymoon Tunnels below Belden. In a few months, traffic for this train will dwindle as Union Pacific, Burlington Northern's archrival, takes official ownership of the WP. *Wayne Monger*

Despite man's intrusion and improvements, the Feather River Canyon remains a wild place with a mind of its own. The railroad is a mere guest that could be locked out or shut down with a flick of the canyon's finger. Thus, in one way everything has changed, and in another, nothing has changed. The Western Pacific seems to be gone for good, and yet as long as a single train runs through the canyon, the WP will continue to breathe. The amazing fact that the WP was forged along the river and through the Sierra on a path that many thought too inhospitable for rails is brought home each time heavy Union Pacific C-Cs pass along the canyon's menacing and enduring walls.

Many of the fixtures of the line's original owner have been removed, replaced, or substantially altered. A radically different traffic mix pulses over this stretch of railroad than WP carried just a few years ago, and with the next round of railroad mega-mergers upon us, who knows what non-traditional freight will flow along the Feather River in the near future. Northern California is a big market for Union Pacific. Gaining direct access to it through the merger with WP was a wise move, one that has contributed to UP's current golden age of profits. The bounty of this market was enjoyed by the sputtering WP, but for lack of resources the regional could not exploit it to the extent "Big Yellow" has. The main centers of commerce for the UP in northern California are the greater Bay Area, which includes Oakland, Milpitas,

and San Jose; the northern San Joaquin Valley, which includes Stockton, the new intermodal facility at Lathrop, Modesto, and Turlock; and the southern Sacramento Valley, encompassing the state capital of Sacramento, Marysville-Yuba City, and Oroville.

Economics aside, UP's takeover of the Feather River Route also kept alive one of the most scenic mountain rail crossings in the United States. The canyon may just be the most beautiful portion of UP's far-flung system. Whether viewed from the standpoint of its heritage, its importance to UP's bottom line, or its contrasts and beauty, the canyon is an enthralling place in which to watch trains.

The distance from Oakland to Stockton is 87 miles, from Stockton to Sacramento, 45 miles, and from Sacramento to Oroville, 66 miles. From Oakland, the railroad heads due south to Niles Canyon, then east into the Coast Range and down into the Central Valley via Altamont Pass. Next it turns straight north at Wyche. In the valley, the line consists of tangents that stretch to the horizon. In fact, the valley is likely the flattest and straightest run on the entire UP system, and is definitely one piece of its vast empire where Big Yellow can put heat on the competition.

At Oroville, a fundamental change in geography takes place, and the 115-mile, uphill journey to Portola begins. Leaving town, the line makes a large left turn and heads up the giant relocation built by the state of California in 1960 to accom-

Near noon on October 28, 1995, an NPOAV negotiates the giant S-curve just below Kramm siding at a respectable 45 mph. The S-curve is part of the herculean Oroville Dam line relocation that the state of California completed in 1962.

modate the Oroville Dam. To begin their climb into the Sierra, the tracks hug the base of Table Mountain, a large flat-topped butte that dominates the skyline north of town. As the railroad continues to cling to the fringes of the butte, it passes the sidings of Kramm and Elsey, both having capacity of approximately 6,500 feet. Just west of James, a siding of similar length, the line crosses a huge fill, penetrates a series of cuts, and ducks under Highway 70. It then enters crescent-shaped tunnel 4 to get past Glover Ridge, and negotiates another deep cut before crossing the West Branch of the Feather River on a double-deck bridge shared with the highway. The right-of-way then diverges from Highway 70 and disappears into the foothills.

While the highway heads north-northeast, the railroad heads due east to hook up with the original route of the Western Pacific well above the portion of the line Lake Oroville swallowed after completion of the dam. At the east end of the West Branch bridge, it enters tunnel 5; and at the northern flank of Big Bend Mountain, it pierces the virtually continuous bore of tunnels 7 and 8, totaling 13,000 feet. This two and a half mile shaft empties the tracks onto the spectacular North Fork bridge. Apart from the world's largest earth-fill dam itself, this structure is surely the state's most noteworthy monument to the 1962 construction project. At the east end of the bridge the line rejoins the original path of the WP at Intake.

Now the railroad finds itself hugging a ledge of serpentine granite with the river some distance below and the tops of the mountains nearly two thousand feet above. At Batchelor Point near Pulga, the railroad crosses the river on a steel deck truss bridge directly below the highway's beautiful steel arch under the gaze of Flea Mountain, and then passes the sidings of Merlin, Camp Rodgers, and Belden. The right-of-way in this stretch is perched among the pines and cuts across the surface of large granite sheets. The geologic formations in this part of the canyon, such as Elephant Butte and Grizzly

Dome near Cresta, emphasize the relative insignificance of the railroad and its vulnerability to the elements. In the shadow of Tobin Ridge (between Merlin and Camp Rodgers), the railroad and highway again change riverbanks. One mile east of Camp Rodgers, the railroad pierces a series of tunnels blasted through solid rock outcroppings in quick succession. These rustic bores are known as the "Honeymoon Tunnels."

A few miles east of Belden, where the East Branch of the Feather joins the North Fork, pine trees quickly thin out and the rock becomes bare and orange. This is Serpentine Canyon, where stone that geologists think once lay under seawater now juts into the sky and makes life difficult for UP because of its tendency to break apart and slide. At milepost 270, just west of Virgilia siding (named for the old Virgilia Mine), the railroad makes a large right turn and abruptly finds itself once again among the pines. Nearly two miles in length, Virgilia is the longest siding in the canyon, and is thus the site of frequent meets. Since the railroad hugs whatever space the builders were able to blast into existence, especially in the "lower" portion between Poe and Keddie, sidings come at a premium in the canyon.

Before reaching the landmark Keddie Wye bridge, the line passes through the Butterfly Valley just past the siding at Paxton. The north leg of the wye bridge heads for a connection with Burlington Northern Santa Fe at Bieber, Calif., while the transcontinental leg turns its course from due east to south-southeast. At this point, the road to Salt Lake finds itself between two fingers of the Feather River, the East Branch, which it has just left, and the Middle Fork. In the 15-mile stretch between Keddie and Spring Garden, the line skirts the edge of the Thompson Valley north of Quincy, and then penetrates a sizable ridge through 7,300-foot Spring Garden Tunnel to reach the banks of the Middle Fork just west of Sloat. With track capacity of 7,900 feet, Sloat is the longest siding in the "upper" canyon.

Above left: Nighttime in fog. Dense fog hides headlights when they're far away, but accentuates them when they're close. As an STNP train prepares to depart its originating terminal of Stockton at 5:30 p.m., the beam from the dimmed headlight on its lead SD60M is revealed by a touch of moisture in the air. Humidity adds to the evening's chill, and it's a good bet the conductor is grateful for warm hands as he studies his car list in the comfort cab. As soon as the carman is finished inspecting the consist, he'll remove the blue light from 6089's short hood, and the train will be on its way.

Above: The lift driver at UP's Oakland terminal is in for a busy Friday night double-stacking containers on an OAAP6 train. Meanwhile, the crew in the cab of C40 9111 prepares to depart with tonight's OANPZ trailer train for North Platte. The OANPZ will reach the canyon about dawn, with the double stack a few hours behind.

Right: An NPOAV breaks out of the edge of the fog that separates the dreary weather of the Sacramento Valley from the warm sunshine of the Sierra foothills. After the 6278 West drops another 100 feet in elevation to Elsey, it will remain in fog all the way to Altamont Pass, 180 miles down the valley.

Below: A maintenance-of-way crew works on the siding at Pulga as symbol BN 137 holds the main. Track maintenance in the canyon is a constant chore, as anyone who's worked there is sure to tell you. In a moment, BN 4252 West will pass over the Feather River below the highway's giant steel arch highway bridge. **Wayne Monger**

Opposite page: Peering over the side of the steel arch at Pulga is roughly the same as pondering San Francisco Bay from the Golden Gate Bridge. It's a long way down to the top of the rail over which an STMET will pass momentarily!

Overleaf:

The canyon is synonymous with bridges. Some are expansive, others minor, but all attract the attention of maintenance forces, tourists, and railfans. The Canyon of the North Fork is an intimate place, which is another way of saying there's not a lot of room. Not a lot of room for trains, for trucks, or even the river. Not a lot of space for the hydroelectric plants that dot its banks. Not much room when you want to build a new highway bridge. No room to spare when you must clean up a derailment.

But the "lower" canyon's tight clearances make it all the more intriguing. In the forty-mile stretch from Pulga to Keddie, it's difficult to miss a train hugging the cliffs or the sound of squealing flanges echoing off granite. Completed in 1938, the intricate arch bridge at Pulga is the hallmark of efforts to make the canyon accessible to the general public. It is to Highway 70 what the Keddie Wye is to the railroad. Without these two bridges, both the railroad and the highway would be up a creek. In August 1994, an MINPV threads the gap at Pulga used by both the railroad and highway.

At Spring Garden, the highway and rails again diverge, with automobiles going over the ridge while trains go through it. Beyond Sloat, the line curves through the Mohawk Valley and the Middle Fork Feather River Wild and Scenic Area. Between Sloat and Portola, the dispatcher has only the 4,900-foot siding of Blairsden to keep things moving. At Clio, the railroad crosses Willow Creek on a huge steel trestle and heads through Humbug Valley and past the old station of Mabie before entering Portola.

For several miles heading east from Portola, the railroad continues along the edge of the Feather. It then enters the open landscape of Sierra Valley, whose many small streams give life to the Feather's Middle Fork. At Chilcoot, where the California portion of the old WP reaches its crest, the railroad squeezes through Beckwourth Pass at 5,500 feet above sea level via another long tunnel, and just beyond at Reno Junction makes a sharp turn to the north to follow the eastern base of the Diamond Mountains through the Long and Constantine valleys. Passing the small agricultural hamlet of Doyle, the line curves back to the right at Herlong, entering the Honey Lake Valley, and heads into the desert of the Great Basin.

Left: 6221 East is one of two closely running hot-shots heading for a three-way meet with an NPOAV at Camp Rodgers. UP and Sprint employees are waiting patiently for the trains to pass so they can lay more fiber optic cable along the tracks here at Tobin in January 1996. The 6221 will stop on the main near Camp Rodgers' east switch, and the American President Lines doublestack train following it will hang back just shy of the west switch as the west man clears for both trains in the siding.

Above: An OAAP6 has completed most of its 226-mile journey from Stockton to Portola on September 12, 1987. Curving through the pines east of Keddie in a section virtually unreachable by automobile except for hirailers, the long stack train will reach Portola about 11:30 a.m., having departed Stockton at ten minutes past 5.

Opposite page: Three battle-tested UP SD40-2s have matters well in hand as they approach Poe's west switch with an OANP. The railroad between Intake and Poe sits on a ledge above the river the builders of the Western Pacific used to escape the Central Valley. One can easily discern that the right-of-way they built follows the winding path of the river and contours of the mountains to gain elevation.

Excitement builds on the beautiful morning of July 4,1996, as an eastbound approaching Spring Garden telegraphs its thunderous voice across the tops of the pine trees. The verdant hues of the woods are deep and vibrant, and finally, down the tangent leading to Spring Garden tunnel, comes a hot train with an ex-C&NW "Lightning Stripe" Dash 9 leading.

Opposite: The air is frosty and the photographer's feet near-frozen as the Canyon of the Middle Fork east of Portola beats with the sound of modern General Electric prime movers. The heavy snow surrounding the eastbound American President Lines doublestack train in December 1989 will become increasingly rare until the cold storms of 1993 literally bury this entire area and force UP to bring in a rotary snow plow.

Left: A hot Ford Fast, WP 3510 West, crosses a bridge over the Middle Fork of the Feather River west of Mabie on November 11, 1980. Much of the cargo has come all the way from Detroit via the Norfolk & Western, Missouri Pacific, Denver & Rio Grande Western, and, finally, the Western Pacific railroads. *Wayne Monger*

Below: Menacing clouds hang over the Great Basin on August 29, 1984, as the WPX speeds toward them at Doyle, Calif. The WPX is about 45 minutes out of Portola, and has a lot of miles ahead of it before its next crew change at Winnemucca. *Wayne Monger*

25

2.
Out of the Valleys

Without question, the Feather River Canyon is a special place. It stands in stark contrast to the topography on either side of it. On the west is California's Great Central Valley, one of the flattest pieces of terrain in the United States. On the east are isolated valleys followed by endless, wide-open, mountainous desert. The canyon is the slit in the Sierra that allows trains to make it from the valley to the desert and beyond, and vice versa.

The Central Valley is the cornucopia of the nation and the world, and is one of the main sources of eastbound traffic through the canyon. In addition to the great agricultural center it's been for decades, in recent years the Central Valley has also become a population—and therefore, consumption—center as well. Sprawling towns like Modesto, Stockton, and Sacramento have become major delivery points for much of the canyon's westbound traffic. A brief look at the Valley and the desert gives perspective to the canyon and heightens appreciation for it.

Above: The elevation is around 5,000 feet, but the Loyalton Branch east of Portola doesn't have any grades that require dynamic braking. This is the high but flat Sierra Valley, and ex-Missouri Pacific GP38 2026 has its consist of empty lumber cars and two cabooses under control at milepost 12 on August 24, 1985. **Tom Mongouvan**

Right: In spring 1973, Western Pacific U30B 3056 and a pack of sisters accelerate over the Calaveras River trestle between El Pinal and Hammer Lane siding in Stockton. El Pinal is where the line crosses the SP's Valley main. UP replaced the trestle with a concrete bridge not long after the 1982 merger.

Above: At the end of a blistering summer day, SD60M 6124 and four other big C-Cs lift a heavy OANP up an increasingly steep grade at Kramm. The eastbound's relatively easy, 112-mile journey from Stockton has just ended.

Top: On a March night in 1973, mercury-vapor and incandescent lights team up to illuminate the flanks of WP U30B 3058 and a companion as they prepare for their next assignment out of Stockton. The WP bought the U30Bs to help tackle the heavy grades of the High Line between Keddie and Bieber, Calif. The railroad had seriously considered buying EMD SD45s for the same duty, but the U-boats' significantly smaller price tag ultimately persuaded management to opt for its first non-EMD diesel power.

The rainy spring of 1995, caused by the meteorological phenomenon known as "El Niño," brought welcome relief to California after several consecutive years of drought. Not an hour after a UP OAAP6 crosses the Santa Fe Railway at Stockton Tower in May of that year, a funnel cloud will touch down under a huge thunderhead, wreaking property damage on Stockton's eastern outskirts.

Opposite and above: Late in the afternoon in August 1986, UP 6036 East is in the hole at Scotts on the edge of the Great Basin Desert. The crew has just stepped down off the big SD60 to give the 2510 West a roll-by. All cars and loads on the west man look A-ok, and it continues its hot pace toward Portola, blasting out of Chilcoot tunnel in a show of jet-black exhaust at sunset. In a half-hour, crew members will step off their C30-7 at Portola for a well-deserved rest until their next run east. *Both photos, Sean Zwagerman*

Top: With the valley's haze from a hot summer day turning the sun's rays slightly pink, a westbound cruises one of many tangents near Sankey. This part of the valley is wide open, with few river crossings or sags, and is perfect for a fast railroad right-of-way or high-tension towers. Hawks consider joints in the towers the perfect place to build their nests.

Above: Although UP's Western Pacific heritage includes thick fog for much of the winter, the traffic it garners in the land-o'-plenty between Turlock and Oroville compensates a bit for the concomitant dangers. Once the eastbound blocking the crossing on the south edge of Thornton (20 miles "railroad" east of Stockton) to make a 1 a.m. pick-up passes Oroville, it will leave the Valley's shrouded flatlands for crystal-clear skies in the canyon and across Nevada. Hopefully, any drowsy motorists in the misty environs of Thornton won't "over-drive" their headlights tonight.

Not long after sunrise, an eastbound charges across the
Sierra Valley at Hawley through the deep snow of January
1993. The temperatures it will encounter out on the open
desert will likely be as cold, if not colder, than those its
engineer and conductor are protected from here just seven
miles into their 344-mile, Portola-to-Elko run.
Brian Jennison

Heading for its destination of Westwood on the High Line,
UP's *Feather River Special* crosses the river at Zephyr on
the outskirts of Oroville on the morning of July 9, 1994.
The beautiful *Domeliner* is beginning the climb that will
double from a constant 1 percent from here to Keddie after
it makes a left turn onto the famous wye bridge.
Dave Stanley

Top: In July 1968, several F-units and Geeps are visible from high above Western Pacific's Oroville engine facility and yard. Note that vestiges of WP's steam era still stand, as evidenced by the water tank in the lower left portion of the photograph. The sizable roundhouse across the tracks attests to the importance of this facility to the Feather River Route, as it prepared both steam locomotives and early diesels for the next assault east. Today, neither the water tank, the building next to it, nor the classic roundhouse survives.
Tom Mongouvan

Above: Western Pacific U30B 3052 is on the point of BN 138 departing Oroville in May 1973. After traversing the lower canyon, this train will use the left leg of the Keddie Wye to continue its journey to Seattle via the High Line. The 3051 and 3052 were the only U30s WP had that employed the old U28 carbody. UP was also a big pool-power player on the WP in the 1970s.

Above: Steel and silver paint are not the only materials that create a bridge between Oroville and Portola. Rock and dirt—millions of tons of each—also qualify. The 1962 line relocation to allow construction of giant Oroville Dam certainly measures up as a bridge of sorts. Its 28 miles include huge fills and five long tunnels. Included is the bridge over the West Branch of the Feather River, where autos use the upper deck and trains the lower. In August 1994, 9551 East blasts through James with a long manifest on the drawbar. The units it is passing are power from an eastbound that's been parked in the siding for nearly 24 hours. In a couple more hours, though, its new crew will take the power back to the other end of the train and proceed east.

Left: At sunset on an unusually cloudy evening in June 1995, 3437 East barrels toward the west switch at Mounkes, near Marysville. Right on the heels of the 3437's long manifest is a short APL stack train. The spring of 1995 has been abnormally wet, as evidenced by the mosquito-breeding puddle in the foreground reflecting the sun's last rays.

Just prior to UP's merger with C&NW, in May 1995, a big North Western C40-8 chugs out onto the main at Charter Way (the east end of Stockton Yard) with APL double stacks in tow. At the helm is H. J. "Hattie" Clayton, one of the few female engineers on the Canyon Subdivision.

3.
Changes Along the River

The Feather River Route is a place of constant change. Take events just over the last decade and a half. All superficial traces of the Western Pacific disappeared, and millions of dollars poured into the canyon like a life-giving river, transforming an ailing physical plant into a top-notch property that tore into the profits of Union Pacific's companion-turned-competitor Southern Pacific. Add to the change in ownership things like motive power and trackage rights, a dynamic traffic mix, and seasons that ebb and flow sometimes tumultuously, and you realize the canyon stands still for no one.

For years, the mainstay of diesel power that pulled trains along the river was EMD's F-unit. Then came the GP35 and GP40 and General Electric's B-B U-boat, and the Fs faded into oblivion. When Uncle Pete showed up with WP's pink slip, four-axle power quickly suffered the same fate. The era of the SD40 seemed interminable—until the C40s came calling, and on it goes. Record on film or simply witness what now appears to be unchanging, because the

next time you look, it may already have vanished. As sure as live oak leaves in the canyon turn gold every October and the level of the Feather River rises after every dry spell, so too the efficiency and shape of railroad technology will certainly change. Without warning, canyon fixtures we take for granted, such as way-side signals and talking detectors, could disappear under the relentless plow of technological improvement. Nothing, not even the canyon itself, really stays the same for long.

The constant changes in machinery only echo the rhythm of nature. The cold temperatures of September and October trigger a perennial change in leaf colors and set the Sierra on fire. Deciduous trees hidden in a mass of pine needles during spring and summer become beautifully conspicuous in the fall. Some leaves turn to rust, some to gold, and some to bright red. The river becomes placid as its level drops, and quiet pools at Pulga and Merlin perfectly mirror rolling stock that skirts their northern edge. But the autumn change in plant pigments and river flow are deceptive. Like the receding tide that precedes the tidal wave, this is the quiet season, and for the experienced it heralds the most dynamic and dangerous season of all—winter.

As powerful as they may seem, 4,000-h.p. locomotives shrink in comparison to the natural dynamics around them. Man blasted the railroad into the sides of granite cliffs and toiled for months to construct several intricate trestles and huge fills to allow 15-20 trains per day to breach the Sierra Nevada. In the bat of an eyelash, the river and rocks could take it all back. And after all that work, there's barely enough room for the railroad to cling to its precarious foothold and operate. Just ask the Canyon Sub dispatcher trying to get two close-running, hot trains up the canyon with another expedited train coming down. All it takes to thwart him is track work at Virgilia so he can't set up his meet there. As an alternative, he's got to hold the eastbounds at Camp Rodgers, one on the main near the east switch and the other just shy of the west switch, until their counterpart can take the siding. Or, query employees like Kirk Baer or Dave Stanley about the winter of 1986, when large portions of the railroad disappeared. Or Don Gulbrandsen and Tom Danneman, who unwittingly probed the canyon's entrails in the El Niño winter of 1995 and nearly found themselves baptized in raging water and mud. Here's an account of their experience in Don's own words:

"Anyone with the notion that the Western Pacific tamed the Feather River Canyon when it built its railroad has never endured the canyon in the midst of a downpour. Man's ability to control elements in

Above: March 9, 1995 is a hair-raiser for anyone traveling next to the Feather River, and soon after recording this train with beautiful cascades above and raging monster beneath, Tom Danneman and partner Don Gulbrandsen made a bee-line for Oroville. **Tom Danneman**

Opposite page: An airhorn whose tone is higher than that of UP's diesels echoes off shale along the Middle Fork as an APOA blows for the crossing at Two Rivers in May 1995. UP's financial foothold on the C&NW eventually culminated in another expansion of Omaha's empire. A hostile takeover of the granger road by the likes of Japonica Partners, L.P., could have put UP's high-speed stack service between its West Coast ports and the nation's rail hub in jeopardy.

the canyon is feeble at best, and the breakdown of UP's transcontinental link is all too frequent. UP invests considerable resources to keep Mother Nature at bay, but sometimes there just aren't enough maintenance-of-way workers, hirail trucks, and other equipment around to turn the tide. Such was the case in the winter of 1995, when I had the chance to witness the fury of the canyon in person. It's an experience I won't soon forget.

"Tom Danneman and I were on a 'circle' trip into the Sierra just prior to the annual Winterail show in Stockton. Arriving in Sacramento by air, we found ourselves in the middle of a warm, intense Pacific storm. Trekking over Donner Pass, we were disappointed at the poor photo conditions, but we figured, 'Hey, this is California! How long can it last?' We held out hope for the following day, which included a trip from Portola down Highway 70 along the UP.

"The next morning dawned gloomy. We found a little sun at Reno Junction and Beckwourth Pass, but no trains. As we passed through Portola, heavy rain started. Rain had been falling hard there for quite some time. The deeper we went into the canyon, the more ominous the scene became. Water was everywhere! The normally tame Feather River grew more intimidating with each passing mile, turning into a frighteningly ugly, frothing, brown beast. Spontaneous waterfalls and creeks jumped out of the landscape. And as yet, no trains—they were nowhere to be seen.

"Turning the scanner on revealed a flood of MofW chatter. Much of it focused on the High Line, which was closed by washouts in several locations. The transcontinental line was open, but the tone of railroaders was frantic. It was obvious that disaster might lurk around any bend in the river. We pushed onward. Familiar landmarks like Williams Loop were barely visible through the rain, which seemed to be intensifying. West of Quincy, a huge pine fell across the highway a couple hundred feet in front of us. We clamored out of our tiny rental car and worked side-by-side with a burly truck driver to move the tree far enough to get by. We got back in the car, looked at each other, and sped off. Finding trains was no longer our top priority—all we wanted to get out of there, but to make it to Oroville, we'd have to brave the canyon's capricious heart.

"I'm an old 'river-rat,' having spent much of my life fishing and canoeing rivers across the West and Midwest. But nothing compares to the river I witnessed on this day! Fed by what seemed to be millions of waterfalls coming down the canyon walls, the river had gone mad. It was the most frightening scene I'd ever witnessed. With every passing moment, the raging river looked poised to suck the highway and railroad right off its banks.

"Near Virgilia, we hit the railfan's 'Mother Lode.' Several trains in each direction had stacked up around Serpentine Canyon waiting to pass each other. Understandably, the going was slow for UP. A hirail pick-up ran ahead of every train checking the right-of-way for large rocks which, like the cascades, seemed to be streaming off the sides of the canyon. At the same time we saw the trains came a lull in the rain, and we were able to record some of what we were witnessing. But the photos can't come close to portraying the feeling of the real thing. Watching the trains roll by

Top: With red, white, and blue GP40 1776 leading the way at Virgilia, WP's hot TOF hustles over the railroad's Third Subdivision on November 27, 1976. After UP took over, it eventually combined the old Second and Third Subs to form the new Canyon Subdivision. *Dave Stanley*

Above: As a hot vehicle train enters Serpentine Canyon from the west, live oaks in full fall color begin to thin out. The colorful trees have a hard time getting a foothold among the rocks. It's a beautiful late-October afternoon, and the Canyon Sub dispatcher is having an easy time keeping 9523 East on the move since no opposing trains are anywhere close.

Right: The tremendous run-off of the 1994-95 wet season is evident as a General Electric C40 leads an eastbound at Tobin. Not far downstream, highway crews are pushing rip-rap down embankments to keep the pounding waterflow from undermining State Route 70.

Overleaf:

The little town of Clio must look like a scene out of a Christmas card catalog on this beautiful day in mid-winter. The trestle east of town is surrounded by trees covered with freshly fallen snow as an APOA glides downhill toward Blairsden. Because of its relatively low elevation, the canyon seldom sees the huge volumes of snow that Donner Pass is famous for, and some years it receives only sprinklings that quickly disappear under the route's warmer temperatures. *Brian Jennison*

in the face of the obstacles at hand gave us a sense of being part of a battle royal with the canyon—one that UP was at least winning temporarily. And, except for sharing it with the railroad people, we had the experience to ourselves. There were very few people traveling in the canyon, very few crazy enough to risk their necks to flood, rock, and falling trees.

"Eventually, the rain picked up again, the trains thinned out, and we escaped, tip-toeing over flooded roadways and picking our way around large rocks on the pavement. Like most of man's victo-

ries in the canyon, UP's was short-lived. Despite the herculean effort of its MofW crews, that night the railroad and adjacent highway were closed, victims of too many washouts and not enough people for combat. For 48 hours the canyon held sway, but then UP beat it back. The storm eased, the crews cleaned up the mess, and trains started running along the Feather once again."

In the last 14 years, UP has created a flood of its own: a sea of Armour yellow and gray that's flooded

Above: Winter 1992-93 brought one of the heaviest snowfalls on record to the Portola area, with several buildings in town collapsing under the weight of relentlessly accumulating snow. UP's Portola yard was also rendered useless by the intense storms, forcing Omaha to send a rotary plow to dig out the yard. On January 10, 1993, the red and silver "monster" rests at Portola after doing its job. At the other end of the snow-fighting train are two SD40-2s for power. ***Brian Jennison***

Right: Not even a trace of spring can be found at Spring Garden on January 18, 1993, with snow piled up everywhere, including on the signal cabinet at the east end. When the spring thaw does come, the abundance and density of this snow will bring beautiful meadows in the area to life with tall grass and vivid wildflowers, and make life hectic for those who maintain the railroad. ***Brian Solomon***

The clouds hanging over the mountains surrounding Poe in June 1995 are a welcome sight to those who bore with patience the long drought of the late 1980s and early 1990s, but they're just the opposite for those who run trains through here. Water cascading down the rocky slopes above an OANP increase the chances of the most dreaded phenomenon in the canyon—rock slides.

In spring and summer, it's difficult to distinguish between deciduous trees and evergreens. In the canyon's relatively late fall season, however, the plants that will soon lose their leaves to chill winter winds become conspicuous. On the slopes above the Middle Fork east of Sloat an OAAP6 glides below a stand of trees that includes live oaks. When the sun drops down low but still reaches the canyon's open spots, colors on the riverbank and mountainsides come to life. Trees and shrubs alike slowly turn from lush green to brighter hues as nighttime temperatures plummet.

two-thirds of the U.S., engulfing the WP, Missouri Pacific, and Missouri-Kansas-Texas (or "Katy"), and in 1995, the Chicago & North Western. Almost immediately after enveloping C&NW, Omaha announced its plan to absorb SP's scarlet and gray as well. Admittedly, UP's paint scheme for freight locomotives is not the most impressive that's graced the land, but it seems destined to become the longest-lived. Notwithstanding UP's relentless onslaught, its merger with the North Western precipitated a deluge of green and yellow diesels in the canyon for a considerable period thereafter. Like a beautiful sandbar in the middle of a rising torrent, C&NW's distinctive SDs, C40s, and C44s added a refreshing but obviously fleeting splash of character to lash-ups pulling tonnage through the Feather River Canyon in the mid-90s. Despite the trouble these coded-cab-signal-equipped units had recovering their air in non-cab-signal territory when in the lead, many trains sported them out front. With the exception of the 8600-class C44s, C&NW units were not uncommon in the canyon prior

to the merger, but after that the lightning-striped Dash 9s joined the transcontinental pool, and they and their ex-granger brethren regularly led freights between Oakland and the Midwest.

With a UP-SP marriage looming on the horizon, the fate of the railroad in the Feather River Canyon naturally came into question. UP announced its intention to hold onto both Sierra crossings, using the canyon for some non-time-sensitive traffic like coal and grain. With its lower, one-percent grade, the old WP is perfect for such traffic. SP's Donner Pass route, on the other hand, is shorter but steeper, with less chance of rock slides, and therefore better for hot double-stack, trailer, and vehicle trains. As a condition of the merger, Burlington Northern Santa Fe will gain trackage rights through the Feather River Canyon, and operate trains on the Highline as well. Suffice it to say that changes keep coming to the canyon just like they always have, and probably will throughout the foreseeable future.

With cutting-edge power of the late 1960s in the lead and cutting-edge power of the mid-1980s trailing, an eastbound intermodal makes its way through the snow at Spring Garden in the winter of 1985. EMD organized the special power lashup as part of the publicity for UP's Feather River test of the builder's blue and white SD60 demonstrators. *Eric Blasko*

Above: Ex-C&NW C44-9W 8618 leads an OAAP6 through
the high-speed siding at Virgilia. The hot APL stack will
meet a hot westbound intermodal here while hardly miss-
ing a beat in its race from Oakland to Chicago. What started in the mid-80s as an experiment has become a familiar
sight along the Feather: APL doublestacks, including tall,
9'6" containers stacked two-high. But just when things
start to appear permanent, something happens to knock
the wheels out from under our presumptions. In late 1995,
Oakland-based American President Lines announced plans
to cease serving the Port of Oakland with its own ships.
Instead, APL cargo for Oakland will be carried by other
ocean carriers. As a result, the frequency of "eagles" in the
canyon could change significantly.

Opposite: With piggyback and carload traffic coming off the
UP at North Platte via Salt Lake City, the BAF approaches
the bridge over the river and highway at Tobin on May 15,
1982. Within a year, green diesel lashups like this will all
but disappear as hordes of yellow SD40-2s take complete
charge of the Feather River Route. **Wayne Monger**

4.
The Edge of Daylight

The canyon is a world unto itself. Sheer, slide-prone, and solitary, it has its own climate, its own vegetation, and its own light. It's cut off from most of the effects of civilization that have left their mark on the busy California landscape. For a good part of the year, much of UP's Feather River line rests in cold darkness. For some stretches of track, sunlight is within a stone's throw, but that's as close as it gets. Bright light paints pines and ridges just across the river in gold, and looking at it seems to warm the soul, but much of the river and rails never feel its direct rays for much of the day until the summer solstice draws near.

Where shadows rule, the mood is quiet, and when they envelop large expanses of water, banks, and meadows, one gets the feeling the day is over. But rounding one of the canyon's huge bends can throw you right back into shimmering, blinding sunlight that will take your breath away! The minerals in the rocks, such as feldspar and quartz, glisten in the low sun, and what looked dull at noon changes to a wonderland of color and spectral reflections. It becomes obvious why the paint schemes of the

Western Pacific included greens, oranges, and silver. Where the minerals are exposed in abundance, they become a natural reflector mirroring the sun's rays across deep pools and into reaches of the forest that have already fallen under the mountains' spell.

The shadows are quiet, the air cool. White smoke trails from a cabin in the distance, covering the tops of the trees with a blanket of haze reminiscent of tule fog. The sound of the owner chopping wood echoes across the small valley, creating the impression that it's the only sound that ever disturbs the quiet of this setting that, at the moment, seems so isolated. But it's a false impression. A few miles down Highway 70, the sun still shines in all its glory, and things are anything but still. The wind hums through the pines and live oaks, the waters of the Feather join their voices to that of the breeze, and the pulse of high horsepower drifts from rock face to rock face.

Up the canyon in sullen shadow comes an MINPV, 7,800 horses on the point to keep its string of loaded autoracks on a roll. But as yet it's just a bright headlight with obscure shapes lurking behind. As though crossing a line of demarcation from apparition to solid reality, the lead unit splashes into full sun, the reflection on its clean nose and flanks surprisingly garish. As the C-Cs blast through a curve from right to left, the Scotchlite on the flanks of the lead unit turns a fluorescent cherry red. While the focus of the engineer and conductor is the right-of-way just ahead, that of the observers along the highway is the entire spell-binding scene. The contrast between light and dark, between the appearance of the motive power and 'racks in shadow versus full illumination, is both soothing and spell-binding.

As the sun falls behind the mountains that rim this part of the canyon, mosquitoes and other insects arise from their resting places in search of an evening meal. Hungry trout jump, sending ripples across the water from one side of the river to the other. Fishermen standing on sandbars bathed in sunlight a few minutes earlier quickly slip into shadow, their chances of success increased by the fact the trout can't see them as easily now. The anglers don't stop their endeavor for another hour or so, and the train keeps on rolling.

Above: The shutter was opened to reveal the mountains and right-of-way east of Poe just after the moon rose over Big Bear Mountain, and an hour later 683 East adds its artificial light to the scene. The governor button on one of the empty grain train's GP40s has been popping out from time to time, resulting in loud diesel roars echoing through this part of the canyon followed by periods of silence. The crew members are undoubtedly hoping the button will stay put this time so they can make it to Portola in decent time and not "die" on the Hours of Service Law.

Opposite page: Freshly shopped General Electric C40-8W 9523 and an ex-C&NW compatriot speed autos toward North Platte, Neb., as the last rays of a fall day strike Clio Trestle.

"Dispatcher Omaha to the 9523 East."
"This is 9523 East. We're just leaving Camp Rodgers."
"I'm gonna take you on up the canyon. I've got some crews working along the right-of-way at Blairsden. When you get close, whistle freely so they can get out of your way."
"10-4, dispatcher. We'll try not to sneak up on 'em!"

An hour later, the forest near the hamlet of Clio resonates with the sound of locomotive air horns. Run 9523's engineer isn't taking any chances that one of the men on the ground between Blairsden and Clio trestle won't hear him coming, and every time he pushes the yellow button on the control desk directly in front of him, he feels more assured that everyone's safely out of his way. A good third of Clio Trestle wears the deep shadow cast by the mountain anchoring its west pier, and only the tops of the aspens shine gold in the small valley under the structure.

"High-ball your roll-by, 9523 East. Everything's lookin' good," radios the track gang foreman. "10-4. High-ball. Thank you much!"

Train 9523's power glistens atop the trestle, but its rear cars find themselves in shadow by the time they cross. The sun seems to be setting fast enough now that a minute makes a big difference. In an instant, direct sunlight is gone. In a few hours, the moon will rise from the opposite horizon and take her turn at shining on the river, rocks, and pines, causing trees to cast stark shadows in the dead of night.

An ORBR with three SD40s headed for the High Line helps reveal the slide fence and two silver bridges at Pulga. Although the moon has not yet cleared the ridge south of Pulga, its soft light bounces off the thin clouds that help keep the temperatures bearable at 8 p.m. on this January night in 1996.

Below: C40-8W 9369 sends exhaust skyward in its struggle to lift eastbound tonnage through Paxton late in the day on September 26, 1993. After the train passes, the big diesel's exhaust will linger, mixing with chimney smoke from nearby houses and cabins and causing the low sun's light to appear as beams through the trees.
Brian Solomon

Bottom: In the area between the canyons of the North and Middle Forks, the railroad runs through valleys, thick pine forests, and stands of aspen. Early on a fall afternoon, the shadows of the hills overlooking Williams Loop have already begun to engulf the lodge pole and ponderosa pines that surround it. The pond in the middle of the loop reflects colors of leaves that have begun to change color in response to the freezing nighttime temperatures of the Sierra autumn, but daytime temperatures are unseasonably warm enough on October 7, 1995, to send sweat rolling down your face. An ex-C&NW C44 whose colors match those of much of the vegetation in the area is on the point of an OAAP6 circling the loop's upper level. The stack train will plunge into cold shadows for a mile and then back into sunlight near the west end of Spring Garden. Shortly after taking over the line in 1982, UP contemplated eliminating the loop in favor of a straighter course between its western approach and Spring Garden. The carrier could still decide to make such an "improvement," but hasn't yet. After voicing frustration to the railroad over frequent delays to its double-stack trains in the late 1980s and early 90s, UP made American President Lines movements some of its hottest symbols. Thus, the dispatcher isn't taking any chances in slowing this OAAP6 down, and is holding a westbound manifest at Portola until the "apple" arrives.

Overleaf:

From high above the rails on Highway 70, you can actually see shadows slowly give way to detail-revealing sunshine in the morning, and then see them slowly engulf those same details at sundown. On a beautiful summer evening in 1994, a westbound manifest approaches the east switch at Poe. In a few seconds, the glistening SD40-2 and two homemade B units on the point will plunge into darkness.

On the evening of April 27, 1991, the photographer catches
Centennial 6936, restored EMD FTs 103 A and B, and UP
steam locomotive 1243 in a tiny sunlight window in
Serpentine Canyon as they descend toward the California
State Railroad Museum's 10th Anniversary Celebration,
Railfair 1991, in Old Sacramento. Behind the operating
and vintage power is a string of tank cars carrying water
for steam locomotives 844 and 3985, which are running
several hours ahead of this train. ***Brian Jennison***

At first, there's only the sound of cool Feather River water splashing toward the sea, interspersed by occasional cars and big-rigs rolling over the warm asphalt of Highway 70. Then comes the faint sound of flanges squealing through curves, a sound so low at this point that you have to stop breathing for a second to notice it. Breaking out of the cold shadows that hide it from the late afternoon sun of November 1994, 6328 West rolls irresistibly downhill with hot cargo for Oakland.

5.
Giants in the Canyon

Ninety-eight feet long. Some 270 tons on the railhead. Two 3,300-horsepower, 16-cylinder diesel power plants. Eight axles with a huge D-77X traction motor mounted to each. Standing 17 feet above the rail, UP's Centennials were the queens of dieseldom. They were a perfect fit for the carrier's long stretches of straight, high-speed track across the Midwest and western deserts, where their 8,200-gallon fuel capacity could be put to good use. Who could have foreseen when No. 6900 arrived at Promontory, Utah, just in time for the transcontinental railroad celebration in May 1969, that she and her sisters would one day regularly run through the tight and circuitous bowels of the Feather River Canyon?

"UP dispatcher Sacramento to the 6927 East."
"This is 6927, go ahead."
"*OME*, what's your location?"
"We're just going through James."

That's all we had to hear. My companion, Pat Page and I, made a beeline from his in-laws' place at Paradise to Pulga, where we intercepted the *Overland Mail East* headed by the "Big Jack." This was the first time Pat, who was in his forties, had ever seen a Centennial in the flesh. It wasn't hard to tell. His eyes protruded well beyond their sockets and he remained speechless for a time as the sleek machine and the two SD40-2s it dwarfed made their way gracefully up-river. It was hard to believe even as we saw it, but unbelievable or not, the Jacks were back and hugging the banks of the Feather River!

Although well past dawn, the lower part of the Canyon still lay in blue shadow. At the eastern edge of Serpentine Canyon, we beheld the first direct sunlight of this day in June 1984. With the sun swung around to the northeast, 6927's gigantic Scotchlite lettering glowed as she led the hot train through the sweeping curve. Although she didn't slack off, keeping up with her wasn't difficult. Her pace was relatively slow, but it was constant. The mile-long string of intermodal loads behind her was no match for her power. Only the canyon's tight curvature held her at bay.

The contrast to what I'd seen on an evening in August 1972 on the south bank of the Columbia River was dramatic. Lynn Powell and I had paced a D-D on the point of a hot train heading for Portland east of The Dalles, Oregon. The Centennial had been doing 80 mph with ease. When it reached The Dalles, the railroad had executed a perfect running crew change, and it had charged off toward the western horizon determined to resume the same sizzling pace. It was a different scene along the south bank of the Feather River. The 6927 wasn't close to

Above: A month before this view of 6914 rolling irresistibly downhill through Rich Bar, the locomotive and its kin were just coming out of the long hibernation brought on by the economic downturn of the early 1980s. Now that the economy's rolling again, so is the "Big Jack," proudly leading UP's hottest train into Oakland, the *Overland Mail West*. **Wayne Monger**

Opposite page: Fresh out of storage, Centennial 6936 leads the first-ever eastbound run of a D-D through the Feather River Canyon. The ninety-eight-foot diesel is part of the March 4, 1984, lashup on the hot *Overland Mail East* passing Paxton's east switch. **Eric Blasko**

Overleaf:

James Speaker's adventuresome spirit is reflected in this rare angle view of Centennial 6936 leading a unit grain train across the imposing North Fork bridge on September 17, 1995. Speaker is clinging to a steep incline that few photographers would be willing to hazard, even to capture UP's last remaining D-D, which has been temporarily switched from excursion to freight service because of a huge traffic crunch. **James Speaker**

80 mph. In fact, Pat and I were amazed that its huge four-axle trucks could negotiate the canyon's curves. Perhaps they were no tighter than those on Cajon or along the Columbia—more traditional haunts of the 6900s—but the trees and outcroppings here at least made them appear so. Fast-moving or not, the image of 6927 gliding through the canyon, like the sighting along the Columbia 12 years earlier, is one that's made a lasting impression on my mind.

Above and Right: Even a locomotive the size of Centennial 6918 is dwarfed by the rock cliffs at Pulga early on the morning of May 26, 1984. In fact, the scale of the canyon in general makes the Centennial and not-so-small SD40-2 3223 look like N-scale models on a huge, superbly detailed model railroad. ***Both photos, Eric Blasko***

Opposite: Four EMD 645 power plants roar in unison through the Constantine Valley with the *Overland Mail East* on August 29, 1984. The D-D's engineer is poised to throttle up when he hits the desert's tangents just beyond Doyle, three miles from here. ***Wayne Monger***

Overleaf:

With the sun still low enough to bring Scotchlite to life, the *Overland Mail East* rounds the big bend along the river just west of Virgilia in June 1984. The enormity of the DDA40X is immediately apparent, since the "Jack" is roughly double the length of, and much taller than, its single-engine helpmates.

6.

A Heart of Stone

The slope of the canyon walls leads one to believe that whoever built this railroad didn't have an easy time of it. What's more, from the combination of incline and rock, one gets the impression that keeping the line open is a challenge as the elements try to take back a right-of-way that took much sweat and toil to create.

The heart of the canyon is made of stone. Unforgiving stone. Half is granite that never moves. It just erodes imperceptibly. The other half is stone that crumbles, where erosion is abrupt and often dangerous. The price for running a railroad through the heart of such capricious rock is constant maintenance-of-way. The following is taken from an article in the August 31, 1990, issue of the Lark, *written by John Walker, and gives a feel for the constant work that goes on in the canyon.*

The Oroville yard office door slams amid the steady grinding of Teletype, ringing phones, and squawking radios. Ray Santiago, the U.S. Sprint fiber optic cable inspector for UP, is here. He'll be my guide up the canyon today. He hands me a line-up and whisks me off to an adjacent office where he introduces me to Jim Gailhart. We talk for a few minutes between phone calls while a steady stream of MofW people come in to toss their problems in Jim's lap.

Ray calls in for "track and time," and we're off. We've barely left the yard to get on the tracks at Mitchell Avenue when the radio in Ray's Travelall begins to chatter. A tamper wants to ride the tail end of our time from Mitchell Avenue to Elsey. The request is granted, and we board the tracks ahead of the waiting machinery. We make good time towards Elsey, spotting a trio of deer along the right-of-way near Kramm. The ballast pit at Elsey is crammed with "Kennefick Green" MofW hoppers being loaded with ballast. Ray explains that the pit is always busy. "That basalt makes great ballast! We even have the SP coming here from Marysville for loads. They're talking about really expanding this operation."

Near the east switch at Elsey, we run into Harry Powell and his crew filling greasers from five-gallon buckets. Harry and Ray discuss swapping track and time so we can run ahead to James. "That's ok with me," says Powell, "but you'll have to raise the dispatcher for me. I can't raise anybody on this thing from here." "Don't you have a mobile tel?" Ray asks. "Heck no," replies Powell. "I always have to have someone else raise the dispatchers or use the phone to get any time out here. You know we're not going to be able to do this anymore after they move everything to Omaha." Ray nods his head in agreement, and we bid Harry Powell and his crew farewell.

As we head into tunnel 4, Ray points out a small section of straight track. "This used to be a full circle in here, but this little section kept slipping away. We finally had to drag all this fill from over here on the side of the mountain and rebuild this whole section up again, and put in this little piece of straight track to stabilize it." Ray checks in and gets time to Poe—time we'll be sharing with a track inspector coming down the canyon. We meet the track inspector near the east switch. "There's a real bad spot in tunnel 7," he reports. "How bad?" asks Ray. "You may want to get off the rail and drive around it!" he replies with a big grin. We talk about how the canyon's been holding up this winter. "She's doing pretty good. We've had a pretty mild winter so far, but if we get another bad storm, those UP guys in Omaha aren't gonna know what hit 'em!"

We continue checking cable. In tunnel 8, Ray spots an access cover setting loose from an inspection port. I hold the panel in place while Ray tries to put the screws back in, but they don't line up. "I'll have to come back here later and drill some new holes," sighs Ray, confused over why the cover won't line up anymore. The mystery is solved when we meet signal maintainer Gary Nielson at Poe. Nielson is out testing the dragging equipment detectors, knocking them down to see if the radio reporting system is functioning properly. "The kids beat the panel up at the east portal of tunnel 8, so I took that one off and exchanged it with the one you found in the tunnel" reports Gary. "But the screw holes don't line up, so I'll go down in there tomorrow and drill some new ones for you and put it back on."

Ray calls in again for more track and time. "We have to meet the first westbound here," he tells me, so

Opposite page: Like Serpentine Canyon, the stretch between Poe and Pulga is an area dominated by huge granite hulks and outcroppings—and it's protected by slide fences. In July 1995, an eastbound empty unit grain train threads the tunnel through Hungry Hunt Peak, with its hoppers strung back around a giant bend in the river. When hard rains come, the mountainsides in this part of the canyon come alive with waterfalls trickling down hundreds of feet of rock. As with many things that are deadly, the exposed parts of the canyon are also strikingly beautiful. But beautiful or not, the canyon's heart of stone is still an unforgiving one, and the engineer is taking his time negotiating the curves just above Poe.

we have a few minutes to talk with Gary. "I was coming in here this morning and scared off a cougar!" he tells us. "He had a squirrel in his mouth and was chasing a second one when I came by. I honked my horn at him, and he scampered off up that hillside over there. He'll be back, though. He dropped his lunch when he went up the hill. I've been hunting up here a lot of times, but that's only the second time I've ever seen a cougar." "It must get kind of lonesome working out here by yourself," I speculate. "I've heard there's a few bears around here. I'd hate to come across one of those way down here in the bottom of nowhere." Ray asks, "Have you ever seen any bears down in here, Gary?" "Yeah, we got 'em between here and Belden. They're all hibernating now, of course, but I come across their markings all the time. One of

our trains hit one near here last summer, I believe."

We give the NPST a roll-by and speed off toward Pulga. At tunnel 9, we find evidence of the recent derailment caused by a slide. As we near Pulga, Ray tells me of a recent automobile accident up on Highway 70 above us. It seems two men in a pickup went off the edge of the road, crashing down into the canyon. One man was killed, the other critically injured and rescued after flagging down the crew of a UP freight. Ray points to the opposite side of the canyon wall. "There it is." Believe it or not, wedged between two huge pine trees on a slope is what looks like the remains of a late-model pickup. "You're telling me the guy survived that, and still managed to flag down a train?" "That's the way I heard it," Ray answers. "The guy was pretty lucky."

Opposite page: A UP APOA (C&NW 8677 West) exits tunnel 32 on July 4, 1996. The rear of the train is crossing the famous Keddie Wye bridge.

Above: In spring 1995, an OAAP5 hugs a notch in the granite near Cresta where thousands of gallons of fresh water, from hundreds of tributary cascades, empty into the river.

Left: Hazarding the dangers of loose, vertical granite, James Speaker ventured up an outcropping through which one of the Honeymoon Tunnels passes to capture this view of a UP westbound clinging to the edge of the river.
James Speaker

Overleaf:

The giant granite domes west of Merlin must have presented a formidable challenge for the Western Pacific's construction crews, and later for those who built parallel Highway 70. On a crystal-clear morning in January 1996, ex-C&NW "lightning stripe" 8608 leads an SCSTX toward a tunnel that pierces a towering "half-dome" of granite. Here, Grizzly Creek makes its way down the slopes between Elephant Butte and Grizzly Dome to the left, while to the right Swamp Creek flows through a culvert beneath the tracks.

We get off the tracks at Pulga and wait for the LFD53 (High Line) train to pass. Business is still pretty slim—three units and twenty cars returning from Bieber to Oroville. East of Pulga, I ask Ray if he's ever heard of the mysterious cows of Merlin. "Heard about 'em? I almost hit one up here one day! I thought I was hallucinating, but they're for real." At Merlin, we meet a small armada of MofW vehicles comprising a track and signal crew. We chat briefly, then head for Tobin. Near Storrie, Ray points out a clump of rocks which constituted another recent slide. We meet up with Walter Steppe, a front-end loader operator who fills in the rest of the story. It seems the pile of rocks at Storrie was in reality a huge, 10-ton boulder that came crashing all the way down from the top of the mountain. "It didn't hit the tracks," tells Walter, "but it hit the fill and pushed it out about 18 inches! We had to call Morrison-Knudsen in to drill the thing into pieces small enough that we can haul out later."

Walter goes on to report that he is not having the best of days. "First I blew a hydraulic line, then a tire, and now my radio won't work." Walter reminds us to stop and see Larry Cabrera, another front-end loader operator over at the ballast pit. It seems there's a potential problem with the fiber optics cable there. The backfill over the cable is sinking under the weight of the front-end loaders passing back and forth. A break in the cable would sever U.S. Sprint telephone service to the West Coast, and if the cable breaks, it will be UP's responsibility to repair it—and splicing fiber optic cable is no simple or inexpensive task. "In addition, all of our telephone lines and signal equipment are hooked up to that system," Ray tells me. "If we lose that, our operations in the canyon will come to a stop real fast."

Larry Cabrera hops down off his loader as we approach. Ray inspects the problem and agrees to have the cable located for repairs to the backfill. As I stare at the huge piles of broken rock, Ray explains that he was in charge of the pit operation during the storm of 1986. "MK drilled down 30 feet into the side of the hill and blasted all this rock loose. We took 3,700 carloads of rock out of here to repair the line." "3,700?" I question. "The reports I saw said the railroad used 2,900 carloads to repair the canyon." "It was 3,700 cars," answers Ray. "I should know. It was one of my jobs to count 'em." "Well, that means that UP must have brought in an additional 2,900 cars from outside the canyon. I heard they were dragging in rock from as far away as Missouri."

At Camp Rodgers, we call in for more time. We now have the right-of-way all the way to Virgilia. The scenery, as you might expect, is gorgeous! Even though I've traveled through the canyon a hundred times in my car, I can't get over the rugged splendor of this rail line. Every tunnel we pass through shows the modifications for APL double-stack trains. Some tunnels even have large notches cut in the roof that run the length of the tunnel. I remark that there can't be much clearance up there. "It's fine as long as we keep the track in good shape," notes Ray. "But if the track maintenance starts getting sloppy, the train starts rocking from side to side, and then we have problems."

We meet up with Belden-Keddie foreman Mike Floyd at Virgilia. Mike and his crew are just finishing up for the day, and I get a chance to see his speeder get put back in the barn with the aide of a hydraulic

Above: A super-hot SCSTX with a single ex-C&NW Dash 9 for power drops down the canyon near Merlin in November 1995. This view of the short train was made from inside Elephant Butte tunnel, which the state of California blasted out of solid rock to build Highway 70.

Opposite: Western Pacific's *Bay Area Forwarder* wends its way out of Sloat toward the east portal of Spring Garden tunnel on the afternoon of July 9, 1982. The photographer demonstrates that not only the North Fork, but the Middle Fork as well, is replete with jagged rock outcroppings. *Wayne Monger*

turntable which lifts the speeder off the track, allows it to be turned 90 degrees, and lowered back down so it can be pushed into the storage shed. Mike tells me, "There's an automatic engine shut-off built into the lift. We had some guy out in the desert accidentally lift his unit while it was still running. He and his speeder went plowing off into the desert!"

Track inspector Sid Moser contacts us by radio. Moser is hirailing ahead of us, and we will continue our journey riding the rear end of his time to Keddie. "Ray, somebody knocked all your signs down between 279 and Keddie," he reports. "O.k., we'll take a look at 'em." Sure enough, the signs sporting "Warning—cable buried below" which mark the location of the fiber optic cable have been tampered with. The poles are still standing, but someone has taken all the signs off. We stop every 50 feet or so and reattach the signs, if we can find them. At the west portal of tunnel 31, I get a quick lesson in the danger of slides in the canyon. I hop out of the hirailer to grab a sign and start looking for the nuts and bolts to resecure it while Ray comes around from the other side. Suddenly, I hear a crackling sound and look up

to see an eight-inch square piece of slate coming straight at my head! I scamper away, running past Ray at the rear of the rig. He gives me a look that suggests, "If you think that's bad, you should see a real slide!" Sheepishly, I hold the sign in place while Ray tightens the nuts, all the while keeping my eyes on the rock outcropping above.

It's pretty close to 3 p.m. when we arrive at Keddie, and the facility is crammed with MofW people heading home for the day. While Ray calls the Sprint people to report the problem at Tobin, I chat with signal supervisor Larry Cobbley. "We've been lucky so far this winter. Normally, we have two feet of snow in here this time of year." I ask Larry about the difficulties associated with maintaining the canyon. "Our biggest problem is just getting to the

Above: Rain is soaking the canyon's rocks and soil, a mere hundred feet lower in elevation, but here in Serpentine Canyon the temperature is cold enough for giant snow flakes to form and plummet into the river's icy waters. 3920 West tip-toes downhill about two miles behind a "bronco" escort to ensure it doesn't crash into one of the slides this kind of weather tends to bring on.

As the camera peers west through tunnel 18, one of the famous "Honeymoon" bores, WP's APRG roars right at it! The train is hustling finished autos, auto parts, trailers, and other loads east for hand-off to the Rio Grande at Salt Lake City. In the mid-1980s, UP "notched" the top of this and other tunnels in the canyon to allow two stacked 9' 6" containers to pass unobstructed. *Wayne Monger*

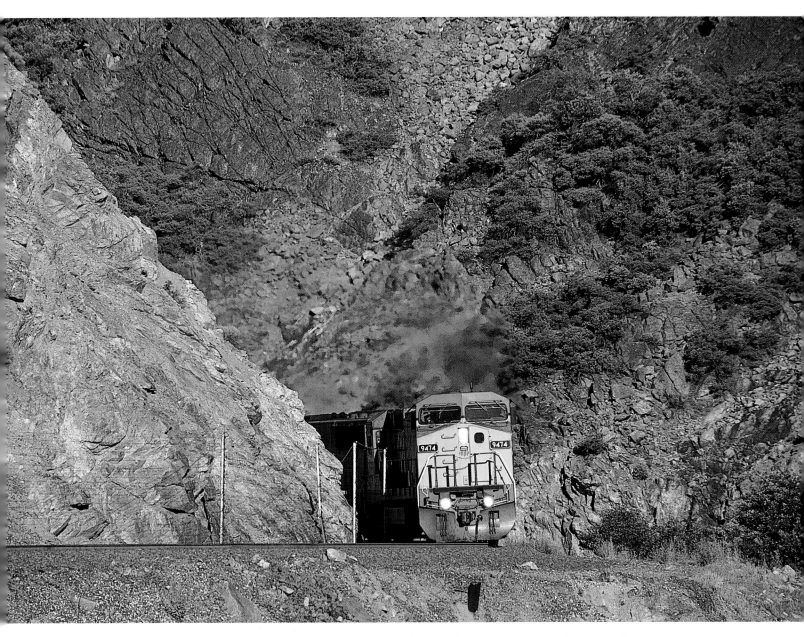

The heart of Serpentine Canyon is bare rock. No pretentions here. Trees may occupy some of the higher slopes of the mountains where enough soil has accumulated to let them get a foothold, or along the river where the railroad has filled out its perch with imported dirt, but the dominant feature by far is serpentine granite. Concentrating the morning's sun like a giant reflector, the huge granite slopes near Virgilia form an impressive backdrop. You'll also notice that the granite is decomposing, which means it could come apart in big chunks any time—and there's not much room between rock and steel in this particular spot! Into this giant echo chamber at 7:45 a.m. in June 1994 booms 9474 East with a mile-long string of APL double stacks. If you look closely, you'll notice just how small the engineer appears compared to his charge. The mountain of rock to his right dwarfs the big Dash 8 by an even greater margin!

problem. Most every other place on the railroad, we can just drive up to the spot where we want to do some work. Here we have to spend a lot of time just getting in and out without delaying any trains. We really have to watch our time and make sure we're not encroaching on somebody else's track and time. It really cuts down on your productivity when you have to spend so much time leap-frogging back and forth over each other's time, and traveling back and forth on the rail to the job site."

We leave Keddie with a clear shot to Portola. Between Paxton and East Keddie, we ride on the newly installed concrete ties; the ride is considerably smoother than on wooden ones. In Spring Garden tunnel, we see that the installation of lights is almost complete. "We're putting lights in all the larg-er tunnels so the guys can see in here when they're doing work." While I've noticed water seepage in all the tunnels, I'm amazed to see a torrent of water escaping through a couple of pipes in the wall. I'm reminded that there's an underground spring located here, which caused the crews who first dug the tunnel considerable delay.

The remainder of the trip to Portola is uneventful. At 5:55, we inform dispatcher Ken Meeker we're off the rail and heading back to Oroville. I was surprised by the friendliness of the MofW crews and the upbeat, professional attitude they apply to their work. They're the forgotten people who keep the railroad running. And make no mistake—they know better than anyone else what a big job it is to keep a mountain railroad running!

The heat is oppressive. Sweat runs down your face as an intense summer sun beats down without a trace of wind. The cool shadows of late afternoon have not yet reached your perch on the edge of Highway 70, but it's a fair trade since the deeper reaches of the Canyon are still in sun, also. The vertical distance from your location to the top of the rails is hundreds of feet. Pierced by tunnels 10 and 11, two magnificent granite outcroppings stand out across the river. With a sense of awe, you watch as a westbound stack train glides along the cliffs far below and penetrates the bores.

Above: As dusk settles in, details of the jagged cliffs above the river and main line in Serpentine Canyon begin to fade. The slide fence protecting the tracks has disappeared into the gathering darkness, and even the unseasonably warm wind of October 28, 1995, has begun to die down. The intense beam of 3307 East cuts through the blue light like a knife, and as it approaches a curve, the fence's strands light up like the coils in an electric resistance heater. You can be sure the crew is glad the shiny strands of wire are in place and vigilant!

Right: Here's the view Dave Stanley's conductor has from the cab of his eastbound, three-piece-windshield-equipped C-C approaching Pulga in April 1994. Nothing but slide fence and rock above—some of it possibly loose—and a large drop over rocks to water below. You get the strong impression that the railroad is indeed merely a guest here.
Dave Stanley

Overleaf:

Right next to the railroad are yards and yards of metal strands, the main threads of a slide fence that can signal danger to an oncoming freight. There's no danger right now, as 6086 East, an empty Foster Farms grain train, makes its way through Serpentine Canyon just after sunrise on June 9, 1994. But is the fence telling the whole truth? On the other side of its thin wires stands rock fractured by alternating hot and cold temperatures and water. That rock could send 135-ton diesels or hoppers crashing into the river 100 feet below like so many boulders. Fortunately, this seldom happens, but apparently not seldom enough. In the early 1990s, Union Pacific negotiated for some time with Southern Pacific for trackage rights over its parallel Donner line, willing to trade the hazards of slides for snow. Those talks brought no change, and UP's subsequent installation of thousands of concrete ties seemed to say, "We'll be here for a while."

Slide! The word's a familiar one on the Canyon Sub. Almost any change in the weather can bring thousands of tons of rock crashing onto the tracks. Ex-dispatcher Ken Meeker was once riding with a "bronco" pilot through the lower part of the canyon. Not far behind them, a westbound freight made its way downhill, following in the path of the hirailer. Suddenly, a voice came over the radio in the pickup. "We're stopped at a slide at milepost such-and-such." Meeker had just passed the same spot! "It was a strange feeling to think we could just as easily have been under all that rock."

7

The Wye

The spiritual center of the canyon lies at Keddie. It bears the name of the man whose vision fired the construction of the line along the Feather when most thought it could never be done. It's the site of the unique bridge that links the Inside Gateway to the transcontinental railroad. It's where the WP drove its final spike in 1909, tying Salt Lake and Oakland by a second rail line to compete with Southern Pacific. It's where "little" mallets, and later U30Bs and ex-Spokane, Portland, and Seattle Alco "Centuries," began their battle with the WP's toughest grade. It's a combination of these and many more things. Indeed, it's not only the wye itself nor the little town that explains all the mystique that surrounds this location. It's the sight of a freight passing beneath your feet from tunnel 31 to tunnel 32, and then magically appearing to the north across the canyon headed in the opposite direction. It's pacing a train up the High Line along Indian Creek as it blasts its way up 2.2 percent toward Lake Almanor and a breathtaking view of a snow-capped volcano. Or watching a train appear as if out of nowhere near Oakland Camp north of Quincy, and then framed by the windows of rustic cabins and new homes—at one point crossing a trestle that looks to be in someone's back yard!

Opposite page: An APL double-stack train headed for Global One in Chicago uses the lower leg of the famous Keddie Wye bridge as a BROR waits at the southernmost edge of the High Line. Built in the 1930s, the distinctive bridge has come to symbolize the essence of railroading in the Feather River Canyon. ***Brian Solomon***

Above: In February 1990, an American President *Linertrain*
roars past the old wooden water tanks at Keddie. The eastbound's containers around the curve to the left are visible
through the pines, where well cars are still exiting tunnel
32 and rolling off the wye bridge. ***Brian Solomon***

Below: It's odd but true that snow covers most of the ground at Keddie in this April scene as WP's *Overland Mail West* bears down on us. The *OMW* is overtaking the 3534 West, otherwise symboled as the *Chicago-California Van Express*, and two BN GP39s that have seen work train service on the High Line this cold day in 1982. **Dave Stanley**

Bottom: A WP westbound trundles over Clear Creek trestle in May 1972, bringing forest products the railroad will interchange to the Santa Fe in Stockton for the completion of their journey to southern California. In a moment, the same train will cross the bridge in the foreground from right to left.

Below right: An A-B-A set of aging WP F7s is making good time out of Keddie as we pace it up the High Line over the bridge at Moccasin. By early afternoon on this spring day in 1972, the Fs will have spotted and picked up cars at Westwood and returned to Keddie.

Below: As a WP local pulls into Keddie yard in the summer of 1952, a family exits the passenger station visible to the immediate left of Alco switcher 563. Anyone who's visited Keddie lately will recognize that a few things have changed since this photo was taken. *Fred Matthews*

Opposite page: All you have to do is look past the A-B-B-A Western Pacific lashup near Spanish Creek east of Keddie to know that this is a summer scene. The reefers are iced and carrying produce from the cornucopia of the Central Valley to hungry Eastern markets. The year is 1952, and the F-units up front have a lot of years left in them. *Fred Matthews*

Right: The *Feather River Special* is certainly the flagship of the entire Union Pacific System, at least for this one day in July 1994. The 645s inside her A-B-A E9s churn their way out of tunnel 31 and prepare to make one of several triumphant marches they performed across the wye bridge in that memorable month. Within minutes, their heaviest work of the day will start when they hit the 2.2 percent grade of the High Line. **Dave Stanley**

Above: On the evening of May 19, 1976, Western Pacific Bicentennial GP40s 1776 and 1976 pose for a publicity shot on the High Line and transcontinental legs of the Keddie Wye, respectively. 1776's charge is BN 137, while 1976's train is the B-PBF, otherwise called the *Bay Pig*. **Wayne Monger**

Above: Ancient but dignified, Burlington Northern A-unit 830 leads the charge as symbol BN 138 roars up the High Line over a structure affectionately nicknamed "Steinheimer Bridge" in honor of great railroad photographer Richard Steinheimer. The beautiful, dry canyon weather on this day in February 1977 is not atypical, but odds are that by the time the symbol reaches its destination in the Pacific Northwest, rain or snow will be falling. *Dave Stanley*

Left: On the afternoon of June 24, 1977, thunder rolls through the Sierra from the direction of the Cascades as BN 139 proceeds south over Indian Creek at Moccasin. The five green and orange B-Bs will handle the symbol to WP's big engine facility and yard in Stockton. *Wayne Monger*

Above: Eric Blasko was sleeping near the tracks at Kingdon (m.p. 104.7) around dawn when he heard the dispatcher talking to the 6930 East departing Stockton. His eavesdropping led him to the canyon, where he paced the special consist on the *Overland Mail East*, sporting the Centennial out front, followed by EMD SD60 demonstrators 1 and 4. On this eventful March 2, 1985, he was especially thankful for the opportunity to record the train crossing the Keddie Wye. *Eric Blasko*

Right: With its bright orange short hood and the faces of its crew members facing directly into the setting sun, a BN 138 lugs the heavy grade at milepost 2.5 of the High Line. The northbound is approaching the portal of tunnel 3 on the evening of August 21, 1980, with its assortment of cars from Southern California off the Santa Fe at Stockton. *Wayne Monger*

Opposite page: In the dead of night on January 6, 1996, a full moon shines through thin cloud cover onto the bridge between tunnels 31 and 32. When gaps in the clouds appear, the moonlight becomes intense enough for you to make out some of the details of the trees and rocks that surround it, but not much else. When the ORBR (Oroville-Bieber manifest) blasts out of tunnel 31 right under your feet, the three lights on its lead SD light up the forest like a flare!

8

The Spirit of the Zephyr

California Zephyr. *Close your eyes and behold what appears: Elegant orange-and-silver Fs on the point of glistening passenger equipment, a train whose colors blend naturally with those of the canyon. Patrons had spectacular views of the river, brilliant rock faces, and graceful pines from the train's posh dome cars. Each passage of the* Zephyr *through the narrow stretch between Oroville and Keddie was a miracle.*

A century earlier, Arthur Keddie envisioned trains running through the Feather River Canyon. To say he was prescient would be an understatement, for the technology of his day would have been hard-pressed to accomplish such a feat. However, shortly after the turn of the century, Keddie's dream became a reality. When you gaze into the depths of the canyon today, it seems impossible that a right-of-way could have been blasted and hammered into being using the tools of the time. Thus, a trip through the canyon in a comfortable dome in the 1950s and 1960s was something to be savored and appreciated. In fact, as the following excerpt from Dave Stanley's article, "At the Throttle of Elegance," which appeared in the December 1994 issue of RAILFAN AND RAILROAD, *attests, it's something to be savored any time you have the chance to ride a Domeliner through this reach of the Sierra.*

When flyers were first posted at Union Pacific's Stockton, California, yard office announcing a series of Feather River Canyon excursions in July 1994 featuring the company's restored trio of E-units, my initial thought was to purchase tickets for my family. This would be a great opportunity to showcase the railroad over which I spend a portion of my working life operating freight trains. Fares were reasonable for the Fremont-to-Portola journey, and I could still get a day of photography in, as the streamliner was scheduled to run a separate trip north over the Bieber Subdivision to the small community of Westwood.

My idea for a lengthy family train trip was met with anything but exuberance on the home front. Only three-year-old Robert would truly enjoy himself, and realistically, he'd be just as content taking a shorter trip behind steam at nearby "Railtown 1897." Now I had to decide whether to join my friends on the UP special, sipping from a cool one in a dome-lounge car, or convince my local manager that I should be the one running those sleek E9s with their 645 power plants reverberating from the tunnels and rock walls lining the Feather River. As the engineer, I'd still be among friends, albeit in a unique way that perhaps might not be repeated. As you've probably guessed by now, this was a tough decision to make.

Setting the groundwork for the engineer's position proved to be easier than I thought. Several hogheads on the Stockton and Portola boards are known "foamers," "buffs," "fans," "freaks," or whatever we happen to call ourselves—or be called—on any particular day. Thoroughly expecting competition from my peers, you can imagine my surprise when Manager of Operating Practices ("Road Foreman of Engines") Jim Farmer informed me that I was the only engineer to request the special assignment, it being a mere two months before the E9s were to arrive. Shortly before the first westbound trip on June 28, three engineers and four conductors were selected to cover the 11 days the special was to operate. Two of my mentors, Kirk Baer and Gerry Lovelace, would be splitting throttle time with me.

On a normal Friday, I would've been on my regular run, the 8:00 a.m. Modesto Roustabout, which works the south (railroad "west") end of the old Tidewater Southern Railway to Turlock. When my phone rang at 8:15 a.m., the crew dispatcher reaffirmed that this would be no ordinary Friday. "Stanley, you're called for the IFMPO-01 passenger special, on duty at 9:45 a.m." Having been held off my Tidewater assignment to operate the special, I took my call and began pondering all the books and videos I'd read and viewed featuring E-units as the power of the day: *Daylight* E7s pulling SP varnish on the Coast Route, stainless steel covered wagons on the Burlington *Zephyrs* screaming across the Heartland and, of course, Uncle Pete's E8s and E9s conquering Cajon Pass with the Domeliner *Los Angeles* in tow. I thought briefly of a cab ride 23 years earlier, the farewell run of the Sacramento Daylight. The engineer was G.M. "Buck" Haynie, and the power was a lone GP9. No, it wasn't the magnificent streamliner I would soon be handling, but it was a memorable experience that helped shape the destiny of two boys about to graduate from high school. John Clark, one of the two friends who accompanied me on that April afternoon in 1971 on board SP 3006, is now a Burlington Northern Santa Fe engineer on the Joint Line out of Denver. If he could only be my fireman today on this 225-mile run to Portola!

Leaving my thoughts behind, I gathered my grip and a bit of camera gear and departed for Stockton

Opposite page: Returning from a trip to Westwood on the High Line, Union Pacific's *Feather River Special* rolls off James Horseshoe near sunset on July 9, 1994. The man behind the camera is the same who, just eight days earlier, piloted the magnificent Domeliner up the lion's share of the Canyon Subdivision. The splendor and elegance of the consist echo the beauty and style of the canyon's fallen flagship, the *California Zephyr.* **Dave Stanley**

Above: At the Portola Railroad Museum in June 1995 you get a feel for what it must have been like on the Western Pacific in the early days of diesel power. Ex-WP Alco switcher 512 is busy giving rides around the museum's balloon track as 805-A looks on.

Right: This is the view firemen had when manning WP's passenger F7s. Although the 805-A now rests at Portola, you can easily imagine the breathtaking scenes they must have regularly witnessed through this wind-shield while doing their job!

in great haste. Phillip J. "Pap" Schmierer had already arrived at the terminal, separated the necessary paperwork, and was nervously pacing about in full passenger regalia smoking one cigarette after another. In preparation for this assignment, Phil had shaved his six-year-old beard—whiskers that would have fit right in on stage at a ZZ Top concert. I jokingly explained to him that he had unwittingly added to the homeless population by shaving, because there were now numerous critters roaming the sidewalk looking for some fresh growth to nest in. As if on cue, the yardmaster came to Phil's aid, announc-

ing the arrival of our train over the "squawker." It was time to get down to business and flag down a ride over to the main line for the crew change.

The temperature was well into the 90s as we waited for engineer Gerry Lovelace and conductor Larry Cope to arrive with the Fremont-to-Stockton leg of the *Feather River Special*. Our patience was rewarded at 11:15 a.m. as a triangle of bright lights shimmered through the heat waves. There they were at last, as pristine as they must have looked 39 years earlier when they first rolled out of La Grange! Gerry climbed down from the cab of the 951, advising me

Above: With the sun near its zenith on a beautiful summer's day, the forest is quiet near Oakland Camp. The station sign and tracks at Spanish Creek appear to be the only evidence that man has made inroads in these parts. The rest of the forest in most every direction appears unspoiled. In the distance, further evidence of man's presence comes into earshot as pounding 567 engines, encased in elegant design and dress, approach with a string of stainless steel cars. The crew and patrons aboard on this day in 1952 may think the *California Zephyr* just as enduring as the virgin landscape they can survey through picture windows, but unfortunately, they're mistaken.
Fred Matthews

Overleaf:

At 5:45 p.m. on July 1, 1994, the *Feather River Special* makes a glorious entrance into Serpentine Canyon. At the helm is engineer—and rail aficionado—Dave Stanley. The passengers he's bringing up the canyon are no doubt enjoying the ambiance both inside and outside the streamliner, and can probably identify with those who experienced similar sights and sensations decades earlier aboard the *California Zephyr*.

As though looking at himself and his train in a giant mirror, UP engineer Dave Stanley catches the head-end of 951 East rounding the canyon end of James on Saturday, July 9, 1994. Dave's eye is framing the streamliner through a viewfinder today, but his mind doubtless flashes back to his trip a week ago yesterday when the canyon in front of him was framed by E9 windshields. Although he never had the chance to pilot the *CZ* on this run, the *Feather River Special* was a worthy substitute. **Dave Stanley**

that I had a "race horse" of a consist, and that the speedometer was five miles per hour fast. Aware of the huge grin on my face, he parted by saying, "Don't have too much fun!" It had been over 12 years since I had scaled the ladder of a covered wagon, at the time a brakeman on the Stockton extra board, and the locomotive was one of Western Pacific's last four F7s. I was considerably older now, and my grip seemingly heavier, so getting into the 951 was no easy task. Once inside, I was greeted by Bill Farmer who advised me that Steve Lee, riding in the staff car *Cheyenne*, would be in charge of the train.

Everything I'd read regarding the Es' redesigned cab interior proved to be true. There was the AAR-style control stand and 26-brake valve looking right at home in this new application. Two comfortable side-by-side chairs and a second speedometer on the fireman's side, an easy-access toilet compartment with strip wall-heater, a new electrical panel, and a large refrigerator built into the firewall comprised the remainder of the equipment. Had Electro-Motive built E9s into the 1970s, this is what they would've looked like on the inside.

Highballs from both conductor Schmierer and Steve Lee were received over the radio, and finally we were off on the 111-mile journey through the Sacramento Valley to Oroville. Passing Stockton Tower, where we were delayed momentarily by a passing Santa Fe freight, we spotted a large contingent of photographers. Each one seemed to be trying

Right: On the morning of July 2, 1994, railfans line the main line at the Two Rivers road crossing. As UP 951 West approaches, engineer Kirk Baer gives the standard grade crossing blast with the E9's melodic S-5 chime horn. The distinctive notes ring through the air from one side of the canyon to the other. After the Es cross the road, they pass below our vantage point among manzanitas on the edge of Highway 70.

Below: Rail photographers and onlookers are scattered through the green grass at the east end of Spring Garden at 11:30 on the beautiful morning of July 2, 1994. 6356's conductor is on the ground for a roll-by, and engineer Kirk Baer is at the helm of the E9s as 951 West goes into the hole for the eastbound hotshot.

Anticipation pulses through the chill morning air at Portola as UP locomotives 844 and 3985 show that they're alive and ready to tackle the next portion of their journey back to the Midwest. Preparing to roll east into the desert, the behemoths put on a show of steam and glistening metal as May 14, 1991 dawns. They and the classic rolling stock behind them are returning from *Railfair 1991* in Old Sacramento. **Tom Mongouvan**

to out-position the other for the best angle under the noon sun. A mile farther at the Flora Street Interchange yard, the Central California Traction Company crew—a full crew I might mention, with two brakemen and a conductor—paused to watch our special roll past with one of their former trainmen at the controls. With the title "Easy Money" bellowed from trackside by CCT conductor Charlie Sherrick still lingering in my head, I notched the 951 and company up to throttle eight as our 1,468-foot, 606-ton, 15-car streamliner cleared the Southern Pacific crossing at El Pinal. In a matter of moments, we were doing 60 mph, the maximum allowed between Stockton and Sacramento. I was quickly impressed with not only the exceptionally smooth ride the E9s afforded—even smoother than the new six-axle comfort cabs—but also the sound emanating from the engineroom behind me. The roar from the 16-cylinder 645 prime mover was almost like the 567 V-12s it had replaced!

After streaking through the vineyards west of Lodi and the dairy farms of Franklin, we pulled into South Sacramento over an hour tardy because of both signal problems and the dispatcher's over-extension of "track and time" to a track inspector. Passengers were boarded, along with lunches for those already on the train. Even my wonderfully resilient mother braved the 100-plus degree heat at trackside to snap a picture for the family album. Soon we were again moving eastward, but not before a second Sacramento stop at the former WP downtown station to pick up a few "misguided" stragglers. Reminiscing for a moment or two, I couldn't help but recall my formative years in Sacramento and the trips downtown with my parents, with any luck timed perfectly with the arrival of Train 18, the eastbound *California Zephyr*. For this youngster, that orange F-unit nose decorated with wings and a figure-eight Mars light remains an indelible image. From the cab of 951, I peered down at the automobiles passing in front of our stopped train, wondering if any of the children looking up would remember this scene in another 30 years.

"Highball, Dave!" conductor Schmierer signaled over the radio. With two blasts of the Leslie five-chime horn, we were off to the races. The posted speed between milepost 141.3, just east of Sacramento, and m.p. 177.5, west of Marysville, is 70 mph. Westbound freights waited impatiently in the sidings at Pleasant Grove and Mounkes as Extra 951 East dusted off crews, boxcars, and stacked containers with our swift wake. With the speedometer pegged at 75 mph to attain a true 70, my fireman, Manager Jim Farmer, began to squirm a bit. New to our district, Jim had never ridden a train east of Sacramento and, naturally, was unfamiliar with the territory. At one point, the speedometer momentarily hovered at 78 mph, bringing my boss to his feet. "Don't you think you're going fast enough?" he nervously questioned. Letting the speed drop just a bit, I suggested we call Steve Lee back in the staff car to get an accurate reading from his speed recorder. Steve's response indicated we were pretty close to 70. He added, "We don't get too excited back here until you're doing 84." Yeah, right.

After a brief stop at the old Oroville depot, now a fine dining establishment, it was straight to Run 8

There's excitement in the forest along the Middle Fork as behemoths 844 and 3985 strut their stuff atop Clio Trestle on April 27, 1991. The two locomotives are headed for *Railfair 1991*, where they will impress attendees of the California State Railroad Museum's 10th Anniversary Celebration with their tremendous size and bellowing, steam-fired heartbeats. ***Randy Woods***

for the 1 percent climb around the western slope of Table Mountain. Full throttle was necessary to maintain the 45-mph speed allowed between Oroville and tunnel 4, just west of the siding at James. Once around the horseshoe at James, we crossed over Lake Oroville and plunged into the darkness of tunnels 5 through 8 before entering the Feather River Canyon at Intake. Operating such an elegant train through equally elegant surroundings had me convinced that I could well be enjoying the highlight of my railroad career. Just five days earlier, I had quietly celebrated 20 years with the industry. At this moment, however, I couldn't recall a single day, save perhaps my first run as a brakeman with the CCT Company back on June 26, 1974, when my adrenaline was rushing like it was today.

Our 15-car Domeliner snaked through the canyon at 25 mph, beckoning the photographers lining the river's edge on parallel Highway 70. It was now late afternoon, and the lighting for photos was optimum. We made a photo run-by—or as UP's Bob Krieger called it, a "drive-by shooting"—at Tobin, affording the crowd on board a chance to stretch their legs and expose some film beside the majestic river. While backing the train during the photo run, I had the chance to try the dynamic brakes on the E9s. I'd heard through the railroad grapevine that they were a bit weak. However, I felt they handled as good as any other four-motor unit which, when stacked up against today's Super Series locomotives, admittedly flounder by comparison. The Es' dynamics were extremely quiet, so much so that I was relying on the ammeter to tell whether or not they were working.

Eastward we rolled, through Belden and into tunnel 24, home of Dave's "wake-up shower." Inside the bore, near the east portal, an endless supply of spring water cascades year-round, providing a very brief but refreshing shower to anyone willing to stick their head out the cab window. Exiting the tunnel dripping wet, I notched up my 6,000-horsepower charge as we thundered through Virgilia, Paxton, across the Keddie Wye, and around Williams Loop into perhaps the best light of the day at Spring Garden.

After a 15-minute stop in Blairsden siding to wait for a westbound unit grain movement, we reached our destination of Portola, home to the Feather River Rail Society, sponsor of today's excursion. As I powered 951 down Mabie Hill west of town, I caught the first glimpse of a Mars light dancing on the horizon from the Society's Portola Railroad Museum. I had been advised earlier that there would be a crowd at the museum, with operating equipment staged to welcome our arrival. Little did I know that ex-WP F7 805-A would be unveiled for this, the museum's 10th Anniversary celebration. It'd been several months since I'd last seen the former *California Zephyr* cab unit, and at the time she was still undergoing restoration work. Here she was today, however, fresh in orange and stainless steel, *Zephyr* wings reapplied, Mars light flashing, and Nathan chime

horns blaring. For this 40-year-old "kid" who grew up watching Western Pacific's passenger-service Fs, this was indeed the consummate "welcome wagon."

As I was standing alongside the 951 at Portola, gathering my thoughts as passengers detrained, friends Kirk Baer and Jay Bell walked up to the power, presumably to take my pulse and see if I'd landed back on Earth yet. They are both experienced engineers, and we compared notes on the E9s. Kirk, who was one of my road instructors in 1988, would be at the throttle for the next three days of operation. Jay, an Amtrak engineer on the *San Joaquin* between Bakersfield and Oakland, shared his memories as an SP fireman during the early 1970s, manning the steam generators on assorted E-units assigned to the *Sunset Limited* out of Los Angeles. Both veterans had been riding a dome-lounge on today's excursion, and I was relieved when they told me my train handling hadn't caused any beverages to topple during the course of our nine-hour journey.

A setting sun strikes the flanks of restored WP F7A 805-A at Portola. The insignia and colors on its nose give testimony to the glory of Western Pacific's fabled *California Zephyr*. It wasn't that long ago that F7s pulled the silver streamliner in revenue service through the canyon. Without a doubt, the feather on its nose is fitting, since the Feather River Canyon was certainly the most scenic stretch of her 900-mile, Salt Lake-Oakland run.

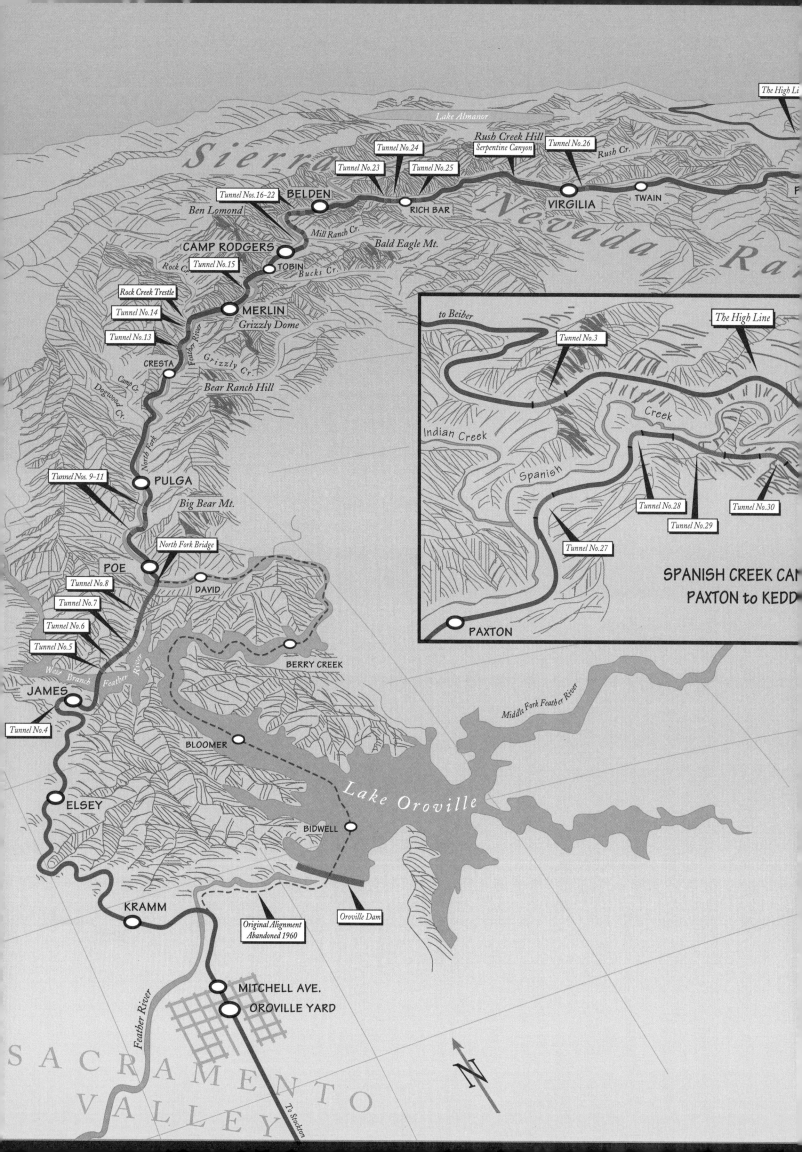